Circos Data Visualization How-to

Create dynamic data visualizations in the social, physical, and computer sciences with the Circos data visualization program

Tom Schenk Jr.

[PACKT] PUBLISHING

BIRMINGHAM - MUMBAI

Circos Data Visualization How-to

First published: November 2012

Production Reference: 1161112

Published by Packt Publishing Ltd.
Livery Place
35 Livery Street
Birmingham B3 2PB, UK.

ISBN 978-1-84969-440-7

www.packtpub.com

Credits

Author
Tom Schenk Jr.

Reviewer
Gentle Yang

Acquisition Editor
Kartikey Pandey

Commissioning Editor
Harsha Bharwani

Technical Editor
Prasanna Joglekar

Copy Editor
Aditya Nair

Project Coordinator
Esha Thakker

Proofreader
Maria Gould

Production Coordinator
Prachali Bhiwandkar

Cover Work
Prachali Bhiwandkar

Cover Image
Conidon Miranda

About the Author

Tom Schenk Jr. is the Director of Analytics for the city of Chicago. He also maintains the Data Nouveau website at `www.datanouveau.net`. Tom has written numerous scholarly articles on data visualization, education, and economic research. He has emphasized the use of data visualization techniques in governmental reports. Previously, he was an Educational Consultant for the Iowa Department of Education and Senior Analyst at Department of Medical Social Sciences at Northwestern University.

I am forever indebted to my parents, Tom and Julie.

About the Reviewer

Gentle Yang is a crossover developer with focus on SNS, Mobile Internet, Bioinformatics, Genomics, and also data visualization in several areas such as SNS data, social events data, and charity community data.

Gentle Yang is currently the senior engineer at TCL, responsible for TCL cloud platform and open API projects. He received his B.S. degree in Computing and Information Science at NEFU in Harbin (2007), where he read computing math, computer science, and Bioinformatics. Before joining TCL, Gentle Yang was a Bioinformatics Software Engineer at BGI, which is the world's biggest genome sequencing center, and he focused on Bioinformatics application building, data analysis for the genome project, and data visualization in Bioinformatics and Genomics.

Thanks to the author of Circos, Krzywinski Martin.

www.PacktPub.com

Support files, eBooks, discount offers and more

You might want to visit www.PacktPub.com for support files and downloads related to your book.

Did you know that Packt offers eBook versions of every book published, with PDF and ePub files available? You can upgrade to the eBook version at www.PacktPub.com and as a print book customer, you are entitled to a discount on the eBook copy. Get in touch with us at service@packtpub.com for more details.

At www.PacktPub.com, you can also read a collection of free technical articles, sign up for a range of free newsletters and receive exclusive discounts and offers on Packt books and eBooks.

PACKTLiB™

http://PacktLib.PacktPub.com

Do you need instant solutions to your IT questions? PacktLib is Packt's online digital book library. Here, you can access, read and search across Packt's entire library of books.

Why Subscribe?

- Fully searchable across every book published by Packt
- Copy and paste, print and bookmark content
- On demand and accessible via web browser

Free Access for Packt account holders

If you have an account with Packt at www.PacktPub.com, you can use this to access PacktLib today and view nine entirely free books. Simply use your login credentials for immediate access.

Table of Contents

Preface 1

Circos Data Visualization How-to 7

Installing Circos on Windows 7 (Must know) 7

Installing Circos on Linux or Mac OS (Must know) 16

Creating the first Circos diagram (Must know) 19

Customizing Circos layout (Should know) 29

Formatting links with rules (Become an expert) 36

Reducing links with bundlelinks tool (Become an expert) 44

Adding data tracks – heatmap (Become an expert) 46

Adding data tracks – histogram (Become an expert) 54

Preface

I am very pleased to have had an opportunity to write this book on Circos. It is a wonderful program that is innovative and applicable to many fields. Oddly, my first experience with Circos, after seeing an article on the cover of a 2007 American Scientist magazine, was to dismiss the diagrams as they were too complex. Yet, I found them to be beautiful and fascinating. I reflected on how the diagrams could be used to tell a story. Several months later I found myself using the program for a project, Visualizing Transitions into the Workforce. The response was outstanding! Lay readers became engaged in the diagram, both understanding the story and asking sophisticated questions. As with any data visualization project, Circos' diagrams were able to engage readers and convey an important story.

The goal of this book is twofold. First, I wanted the book to be accessible to all users who have an interest in displaying data and relationships to a broad audience. In my experience, many users—particularly those using Windows—become frustrated when trying to install and create their first diagram.

Secondly, I want to show how Circos can be used in the social sciences even though the program's roots are in Bioinformatics, specifically Genetics. It is a powerful tool for social sciences, including Political Science, Economics, Education, and other fields.

I hope you enjoy this book and Circos.

What this book covers

Installing Circos on Windows 7 (Must know), explains one of the most challenging aspects of Circos, which is to install and run on the Windows operating system. We will walk through the installation process by showing each step. The recipe also highlights how each step is necessary to create the Circos diagram, and discusses common issues and solutions typically seen during installation.

Installing Circos on Linux or Mac OS (Must know), discusses each step needed to install Circos on a Linux or Mac OS X operating system. Despite the variety of Linux operating systems, the recipe demonstrates the installation process solely through commands in the Terminal window. It highlights issues typically faced during installation for Linux users, and their solutions, just like the previous recipe does for Windows users.

Creating the first Circos diagram (Must know), shows you how to create a basic diagram in Circos after installation, to show the basic relationships with ribbons. This recipe also shows you how to transform survey data in a proper format to be used for Circos. It discusses each step needed to create a new visualization.

Customizing Circos layout (Should know), discusses how to adjust which data to plot, adding and customizing labels, and adding tick marks. The appearance of a Circos diagram is highly customizable. As an example, this recipe uses political contributions from each U.S. State to trace and investigate the patterns.

Formatting links with rules (Become an expert), shows you how we can use rules to help illuminate the important data though Circos can display a lot of data in a single diagram. It also shows you how to use rules to adjust the size of ribbons and change their colors and transparency.

Reducing links with bundlelinks tool (Become an expert), discusses how Circos' bundlelinks tool can be used to reduce the number of ribbons and links to enhance readability. Sometimes the users have to deal with too much data to be plotted in a single diagram; this recipe helps the readers to manage the data in such cases.

Adding data tracks – heatmap (Become an expert), shows you how to add additional layers of data in your diagram. It further explores political contributions by adding a heatmap to your diagram and talks about how to change the colors by using the popular Colorbrewer palettes.

Adding data tracks – histogram (Become an expert), discusses how to include histograms to our diagrams, as heatmaps are not the only way to display additional data. The final diagram, which reflects the collective progress throughout the book, will display five dimensions of data (political parties, states, donations, donations per capita, and the recipient's office) on a single plot.

What you need for this book

You will need a computer running Windows (XP, Vista, Windows 7, or Windows 8), Mac OS X, or Linux. You will need the Circos program and Perl (the installation of these programs are covered in the book). Likewise, you will need an active Internet connection during the installation process. Most of all, you will need patience.

Who this book is for

This book is targeted towards those who are unfamiliar with Circos, irrespective of their professional background. The author does not presume any familiarity with Perl or even the Windows Command Prompt or Terminal. Nevertheless, the author presumes the reader is able to navigate through folders and directories. However, the intermediate and advanced users will also be able to learn how to create and customize Circos diagrams.

Conventions

In this book, you will find a number of styles of text that distinguish between different kinds of information. Here are some examples of these styles, and an explanation of their meaning.

Code words in text are shown as follows: "Rename this folder as `Circos` and move it to `C:\Program Files (x86)\`."

A block of code is set as follows:

```
<colors>
<<include colors.conf>>
<<include C:\Program Files (x86)\Circos\etc\colors.conf>>
</colors>
<fonts>
<<include C:\Program Files (x86)\Circos\etc\fonts.conf>>
</fonts>
```

When we wish to draw your attention to a particular part of a code block, the relevant lines or items are set in bold:

```
<image>
dir = C:\Users\tls573\Dropbox\Circos Data Visualization Book\Book\
4 - Data tracks\data
file  = ElectionContributions-heatmap
svg = yes
png = yes
```

Any command-line input or output is written as follows:

```
cd ~/
mv circos-X.XX Circos
```

New terms and **important words** are shown in bold. Words that you see on the screen, in menus or dialog boxes for example, appear in the text like this: "Click on the **Start** menu and then right-click on **Computer**."

> Warnings or important notes appear in a box like this.

> Tips and tricks appear like this.

Reader feedback

Feedback from our readers is always welcome. Let us know what you think about this book—what you liked or may have disliked. Reader feedback is important for us to develop titles that you really get the most out of.

To send us general feedback, simply send an e-mail to `feedback@packtpub.com`, and mention the book title via the subject of your message.

If there is a book that you need and would like to see us publish, please send us a note in the **SUGGEST A TITLE** form on `www.packtpub.com` or e-mail `suggest@packtpub.com`.

If there is a topic that you have expertise in and you are interested in either writing or contributing to a book, see our author guide on `www.packtpub.com/authors`.

Customer support

Now that you are the proud owner of a Packt book, we have a number of things to help you to get the most from your purchase.

Downloading the example code

You can download the example code files for all Packt books you have purchased from your account at `http://www.PacktPub.com`. If you purchased this book elsewhere, you can visit `http://www.PacktPub.com/support` and register to have the files e-mailed directly to you.

Downloading the color images of this book

We also provide you a PDF file that has color images of the screenshots used in this book. The color images will help you better understand the changes in the output. You can download this file from `http://www.packtpub.com/sites/default/files/downloads/4407OT_Images.pdf`.

Errata

Although we have taken every care to ensure the accuracy of our content, mistakes do happen. If you find a mistake in one of our books—maybe a mistake in the text or the code—we would be grateful if you would report this to us. By doing so, you can save other readers from frustration and help us improve subsequent versions of this book. If you find any errata, please report them by visiting `http://www.packtpub.com/support`, selecting your book, clicking on the **errata submission form** link, and entering the details of your errata. Once your errata are verified, your submission will be accepted and the errata will be uploaded on our website, or added to any list of existing errata, under the Errata section of that title. Any existing errata can be viewed by selecting your title from `http://www.packtpub.com/support`.

Piracy

Piracy of copyright material on the Internet is an ongoing problem across all media. At Packt, we take the protection of our copyright and licenses very seriously. If you come across any illegal copies of our works, in any form, on the Internet, please provide us with the location address or website name immediately so that we can pursue a remedy.

Please contact us at `copyright@packtpub.com` with a link to the suspected pirated material.

We appreciate your help in protecting our authors, and our ability to bring you valuable content.

Questions

You can contact us at `questions@packtpub.com` if you are having a problem with any aspect of the book, and we will do our best to address it.

Circos Data Visualization How-to

Circos is a program designed to display genetic, tabular, and categorical data in a visually pleasing circular diagram. It is a set of Perl files, without any graphical user interface. Although powerful, the lack of a graphical user interface can perplex novice and intermediate users. This short book will walk you through installing the software and creating images. Circos was originally used to graph genetic data, but we will walk through examples from the social sciences that have a broader appeal.

Installing Circos on Windows 7 (Must know)

Let's walk through the installation of Circos and the necessary **Perl** modules to our computer. Circos requires a few different components to work. These include Circos and Circos tools by Martin Krzywinski, the Perl programming language, which interprets Circos' actions, and a few additional Perl modules. In this recipe, we will go through each step to install the necessary files onto our computer.

Getting ready

We will need to use a few tools during the installation process; software to extract the Circos installation files and the Windows Command Prompt to install those files. If you are a professional Perl developer, you may want to skip to the next section.

Circos is downloadable through a tarball. A **tarball** (which produces the archive in the formats `.tar`, `.gz`, or `.tgz`) compresses larger files into a smaller folder—similar to a ZIP folder. But unlike a ZIP folder, it is not compatible with Windows built-in tools, so we will need to download another program. We will use 7-Zip—a free, non-intrusive software package—to uncompress our files.

Before downloading any Circos files, go to at `www.7-zip.org`, then download and install the program on your computer. We will also heavily use the Windows Command Prompt during the installation and utilization of Circos. The fastest way to access the Command Prompt is to type *Windows + R* to bring up the **Run...** menu. It will look something like the next screenshot. Type `cmd \` and hit *Enter* or click on **OK** to bring up the prompt.

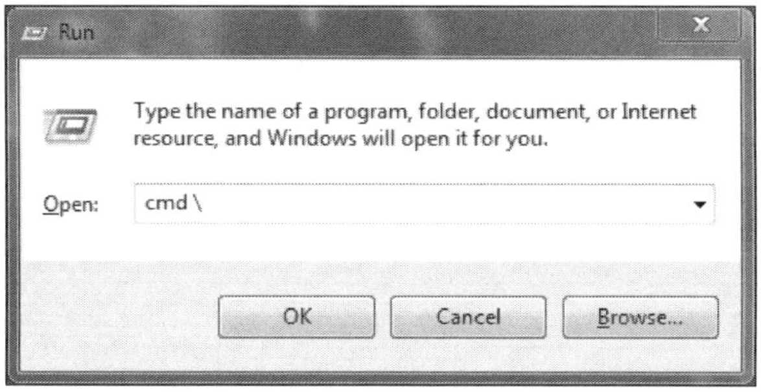

> Not sure whether you need a 32-bit or a 64-bit version? See the *Do I need a 32-bit or 64-bit version?* section ahead. If that is too time-consuming, you can download the 32-bit version, which is compatible with both 32-bit and 64-bit operating systems.

A new, predominantly black window will appear with the Command Prompt as shown in the following screenshot. We will type commands in the prompt at various stages. Anytime this tutorial mentions the Command Prompt, we can access it by typing *Windows + R* and type `cmd \`.

How to do it...

1. Download Circos by visiting `circos.ca/software/download/` and downloading `circos-X.XX.tgz` and `circos-tools-X.XX.tgz`, where `X.XX` is the version number. The version numbers for Circos and Circos tools are not the same.
2. Extract the **circos-X.XX.tgz** into a folder using 7-Zip or any other compatible software program. Extracting the files using 7-Zip is a two-step procedure.
3. Right-click on **circos-X.XX.tgz**, choose the **7-Zip** menu, and click on **Extract Here**. This will create another file called **circos-X.XX.tar**. The next screenshot shows you this process:

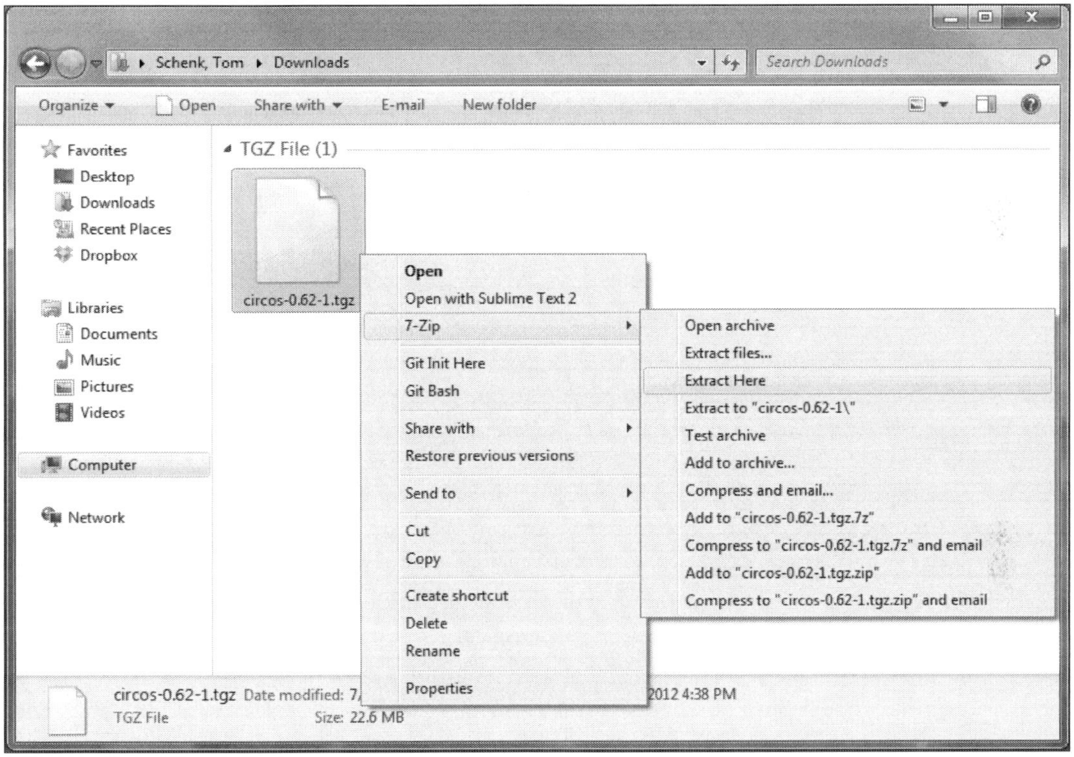

The next screenshot shows the extracted file:

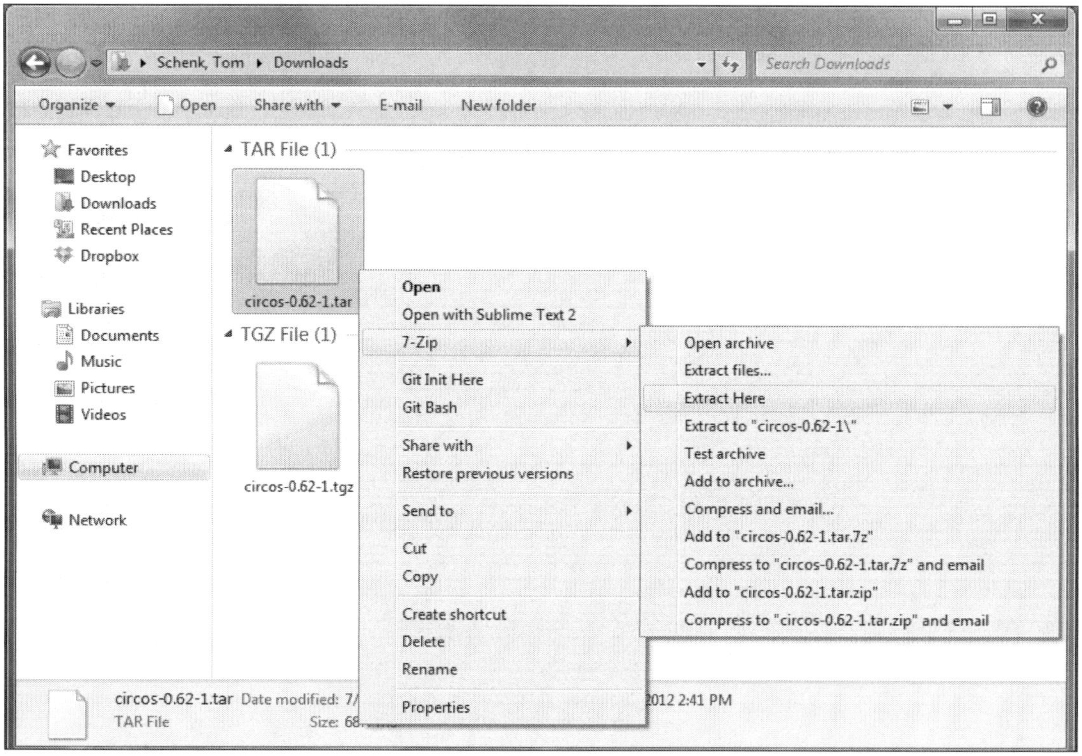

4. We need to extract this file further again by right-clicking on the file, choosing the **7-Zip** menu, and selecting **Extract Here**.

   Finally, you will be presented with a folder labeled `circos-X.XX`, which contains several folders and files within it. These are the Circos files that are used to create a diagram.

5. Rename this folder as `Circos` and move it to `C:\Program Files (x86)\`. This will be the installation location for Circos. Move the extracted folder into its own directory that is `C:\Program Files (x86)`, and rename it. For this tutorial, the Circos files are contained in `C:\Program Files (x86)\Circos\`.

> Not able to find `C:\Program Files (x86)`? Earlier versions (for example, Windows XP) or the 32-bit version of Windows uses `C:\Program Files`. Simply use the `C:\Program Files` directory for this book.

6. Extract the `circos-tools-X.XX.tgz` file using the same methods as previously mentioned: right-click on the file, choose **7-Zip**, and select **Extract Here**. This will generate a `circos-tools-X.XX.tar` file; select it, choose **7-Zip**, and select **Extract Here** again.
7. Rename the `circos-tools-X.XX` folder to `Circos Tools`. Then move the `Circos Tools` folder to the Circos installation folder (for example, `C:\Program Files (x86)\Circos`). Circos tools will be located at `C:\Program Files (x86)\Circos\Circos Tools`.
8. Now we need to install Perl on our computer. We will use Strawberry Perl for our Windows installation. Install Strawberry Perl—a free Windows-compatible version of Perl—on your computer by visiting `strawberryperl.com`.
9. Choose either the 64-bit or the 32-bit installation for your computer. If you want to move quickly choose the 32-bit version.
10. Execute the installer and walk through the menu. Use the default suggestions.
11. Ensure Perl is correctly installed by opening the Windows Command Prompt (see the *Getting Started* section), and then type `perl -v`. You should see some text beginning with **This is perl**. If you're greeted with **not recognized as an internal or external command**, see the *I installed Perl but perl -v doesn't work!* section ahead.

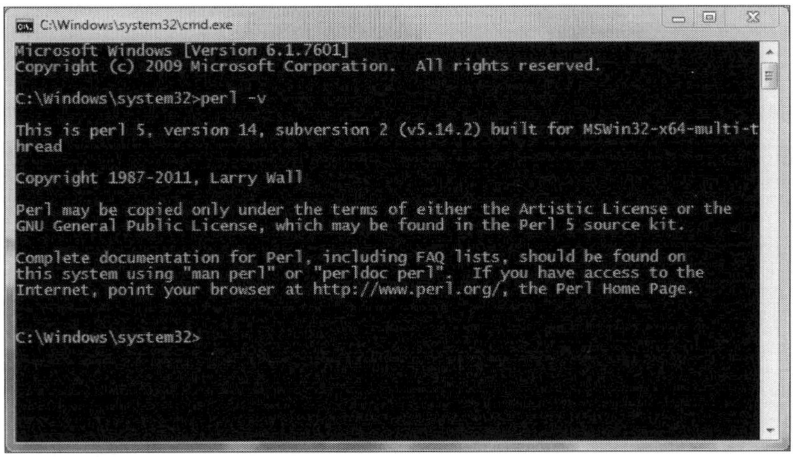

12. Next we need to install some additional Perl modules needed by Circos to create diagrams. In the Command Prompt, copy and paste (or type) the following command:

```
cpan Config::General GD GD::Polyline List::MoreUtils Math::Bezier
Math::Round Math::VecStat Params::Validate Readonly Regexp::Common
Set::IntSpan Text::Format Clone Font::TTF Statistics::Descriptive
```

    The Command Prompt will scroll through lines of text as the modules are downloaded and installed to your computer. Once this concludes, it means that the installation of Circos, Perl, and the necessary modules has been completed.

Running an example

Let's check to make sure our installation of Circos and Perl were done correctly, by compiling an example image. In the Windows Command Prompt, type the following commands:

```
cd C:\Program Files (x86)\Circos\example

perl "C:\Program Files (x86)\Circos\bin\circos" -conf "example\etc\
circos.conf"
```

After a brief pause, several dozen lines of text will scroll down the Command Prompt as various elements are "drawn" for the image. If anything is incorrect, you will see a noticeable error appearing in the window. Otherwise you will see a summary of the time elapsed to make the image, similar to what is shown in next screenshot:

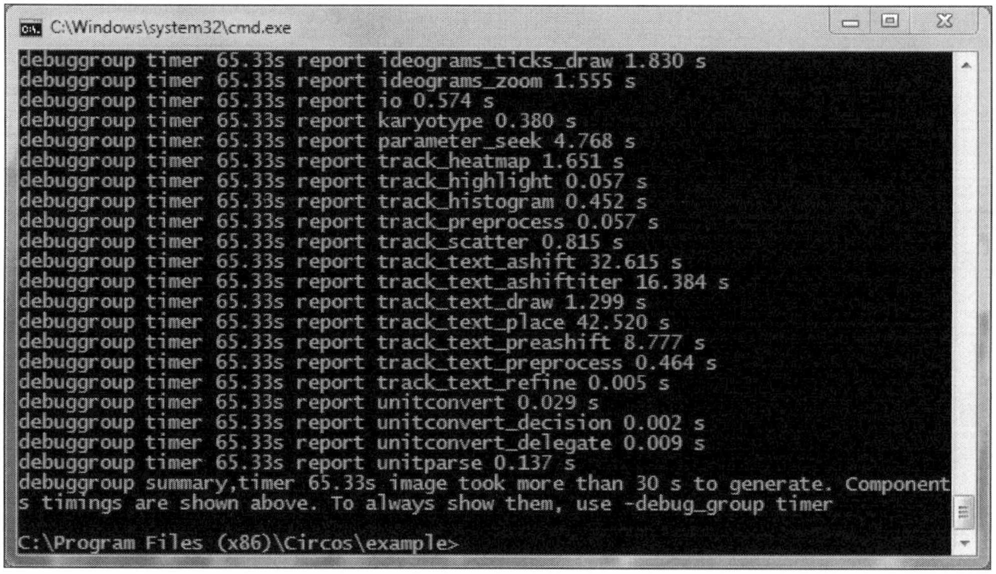

In Windows Explorer, navigate to `C:\Program Files (x86)\Circos\example` and open `circos.png` to view the successful output.

Do I need a 64-bit or a 32-bit version?

Computers are available in two versions of Windows operating systems—64-bit and 32-bit. 64-bit machines are becoming common as they are able to store additional memory. Programs also come in 32-bit and 64-bit versions. A 32-bit program will run on a 64-bit computer, but a 64-bit program cannot run on a 32-bit computer, that is, the newest version can run the older version but the older version, obviously, cannot run the new version.

You can check to see which type you have. Click on the **Start** menu and then right-click on **Computer**. Look at the following screenshot:

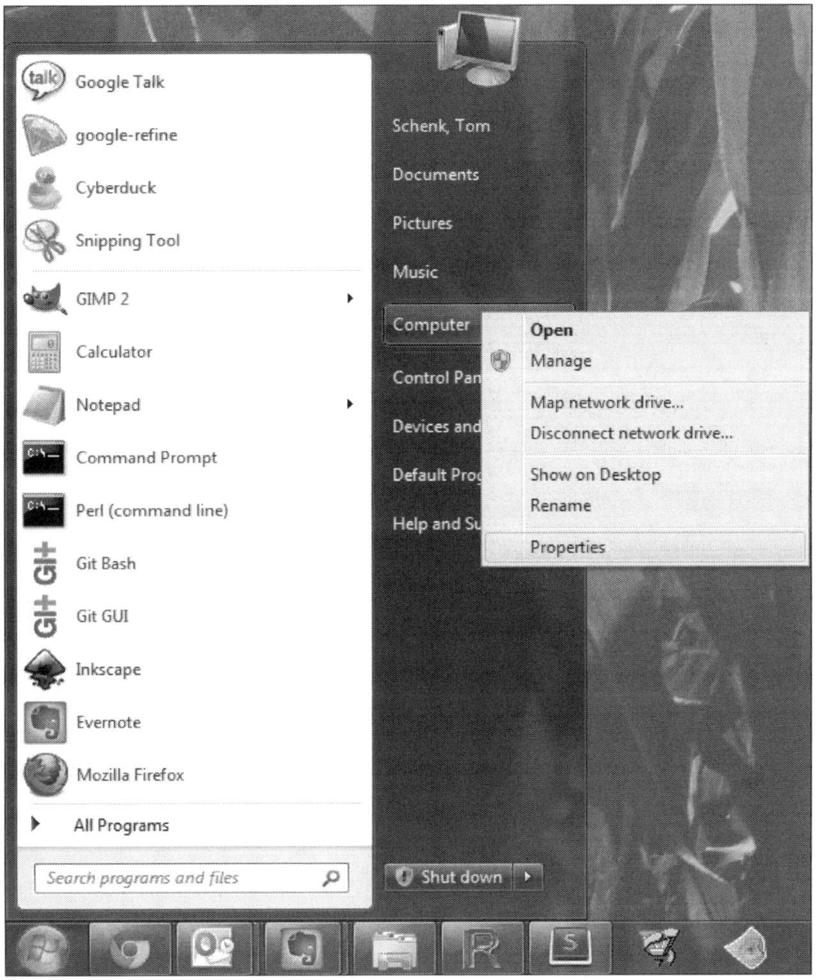

Next to **System type**, your computer will list if it's a 32-bit or 64-bit operating system as shown in the next screenshot:

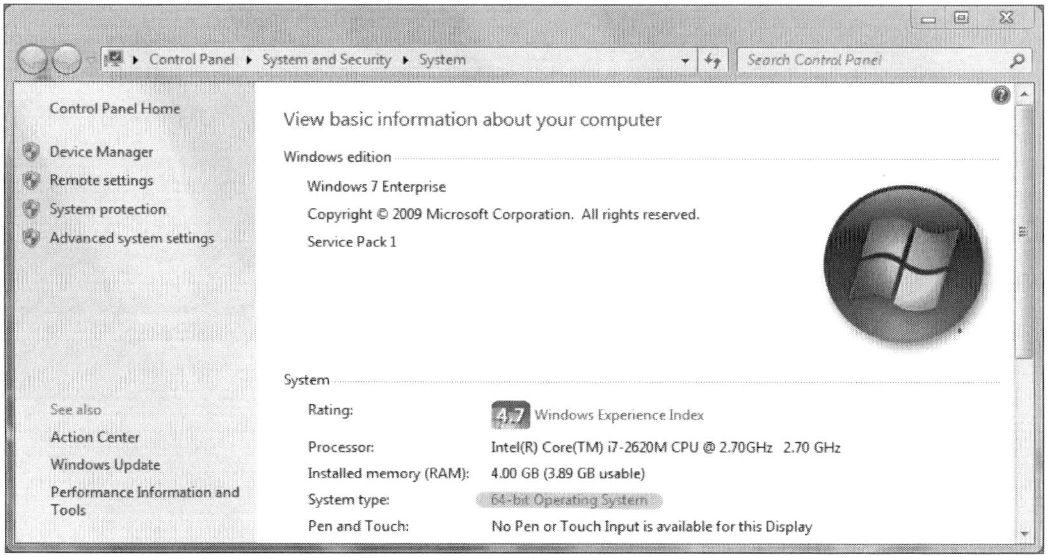

But why is there a difference? 32-bit machines, due to some underlying mathematics, cannot read more than 4 GB of RAM—regardless of how much you have in your machine. The current 64-bit Windows operating systems can access between 16 GB and 192 GB of RAM, while theoretically they can access 1 billion times 17.2 GB. This is notable for those who work with "big data" and need lots of memory.

I want Circos, what is Perl?

Circos is not a standalone program. It is a collection of files that use the Perl programming language and modules to build a graph. So the installation comes in multiple parts. First, install Circos; secondly, install Perl, and then install the additional Perl modules that extend the functionality of Perl even further.

When we run Circos, the program will take our data and call upon Perl to create the diagram. In effect, every computer program operates on a similar logic; it takes what you want and explains how to do it in a particular programming language. Usually, everything is presented in a standalone program, so you don't have to mess with both sides.

What are Perl modules?

Perl modules extend the functionality of the language and are often written by other users. Each module is stored in the **Comprehensive Perl Archive Network** (**CPAN**)—a sort of app store containing Perl modules. We can access and install these modules through the command window by typing `cpan`, and then typing each package we want to install separated by a space.

Circos requires a dozen Perl modules; but diligent readers may have noticed we installed 14 modules. Strawberry Perl is only packaged with a handful of modules, so this is why we needed to install a few more.

I installed Perl, but perl -v does not work!

Perl is installed to your computer and we can usually execute it by typing `perl` in the command window. Sometimes this does not work because Windows does not know where we installed Perl. Usually, we just need to be sure Perl is contained in something called **Windows Path**.

Click on the **Start** menu and then right-click on **Computer** to open your computer's **Properties** window. Click on **Advanced system settings** and then, in the new dialog box, choose the **Environmental Variables...** button near the bottom. The next screenshot is what you see during this procedure:

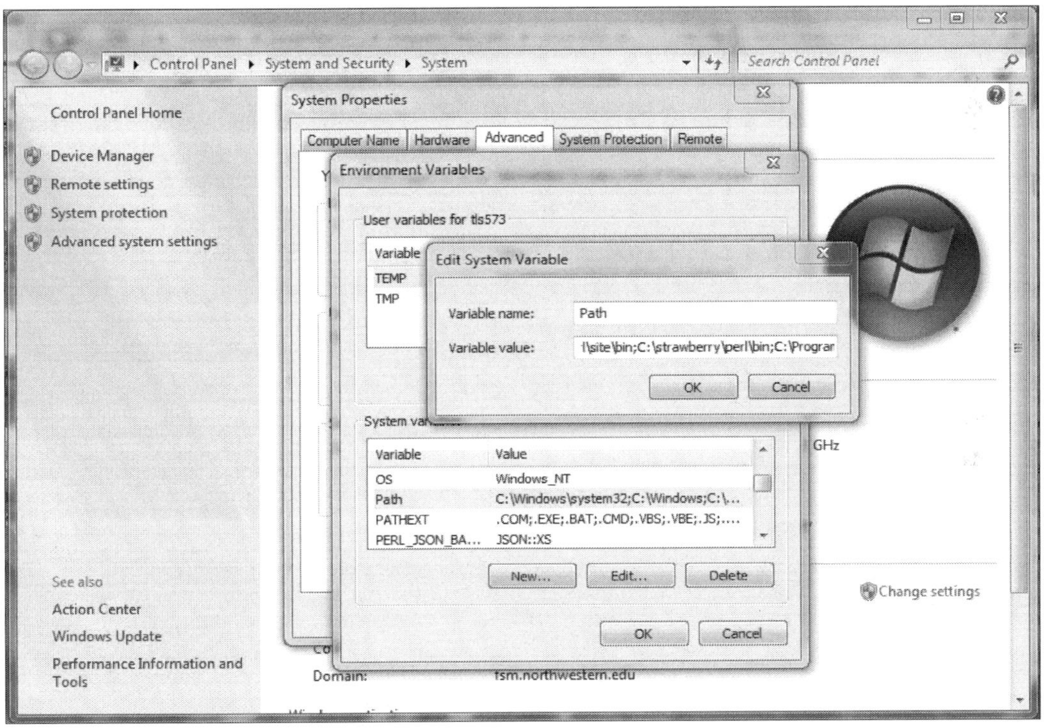

Use the box at the bottom to scroll to the **Path** variable, select that line, and click on **Edit...**. The value of this variable will contain multiple file paths separated by a semicolon. Scroll across to see if your Perl installation is listed (usually listed as **C:\Strawberry\c\bin**). If not, manually type the location of the installation.

Installing Circos under Cygwin

Advanced users may want to install Circos under Cygwin. The Cygwin lets Windows mimic the Linux environment, adding both power and complexity. Presumably, Cygwin users are more computer savvy and may have entirely skipped this section. But if Cygwin interests you, install Cygwin using their instructions, and install Circos using the instructions for Linux contained in this recipe. If you have not worked with Linux in the past, I would recommend sticking to the installation instructions mentioned in the previous section.

Installing Circos on Linux or Mac OS (Must know)

We will walk through the installation of Circos on Linux, specifically on the Debian-based Linux Mint. This section will use the terminal interface and, at times, the web browser, which means the instructions can be generalized to other Linux- and Unix-based distributions such as Mac OS.

Getting ready

The easiest way to utilize Circos is on a Linux- or Unix-based distribution. Many of the creator's tutorials and documentation focus on executive Linux terminal commands and usually rely on built-in tools. We will need to install several components, including the Circos files, the Perl programming language, and some additional Perl modules.

We will rely on the terminal for installation, so find and open it.

How to do it...

Download Circos by visiting `circos.ca/software/download/` and downloading `circos-X.XX.tgz` and `circos-tools-X.XX.tgz`, where `X.XX` is the version number. The version number for Circos and Circos tools is not the same.

1. Open the **Terminal** window and change the directory to the location of the download as follows:

   ```
   cd ~/Downloads
   ```

2. Extract the folder with the following command:

   ```
   tar xvfz circos-X.XX.tgz
   ```

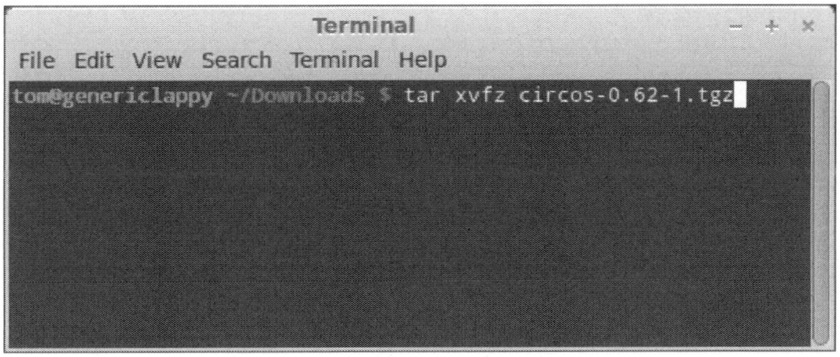

3. Move the folder (not yet extracted) to the desired directory in the user's home directory using the following command:

```
mv circos-X.XX ~/
```

4. Now rename the Circos directory to be consistent with the other installations shown in this book. This can be done as follows:

```
cd ~/
mv circos-X.XX Circos
```

5. Extract the Circos tools' tarball and move it to the location of your Circos installation by using the following commands:

```
cd ~/Downloads
tar xvfz circos-tools-X.XX.tgz
mv circos-tools-X.XX ~/Circos
mv ~/Circos/circos-tools-X.XX ~/Circos/Circos Tools
```

6. Install the necessary Perl modules by typing the following command into the **Terminal** window:

```
cpan config::General GD GD::Polyline List::MoreUtils Math::Bezier
Math::Round Math::VecStat Params::Validate Readonly Regexp::Common
Set::IntSpan Text::Format Clone Font::TTF Statistics::Descriptive
```

7. The command in the **Terminal** window may ask to automate the installation process; choose yes (type `y`). It will also ask how it wants you to install; type `sudo`. Finally, it will ask if you want it to choose the mirror; simply type `yes`.

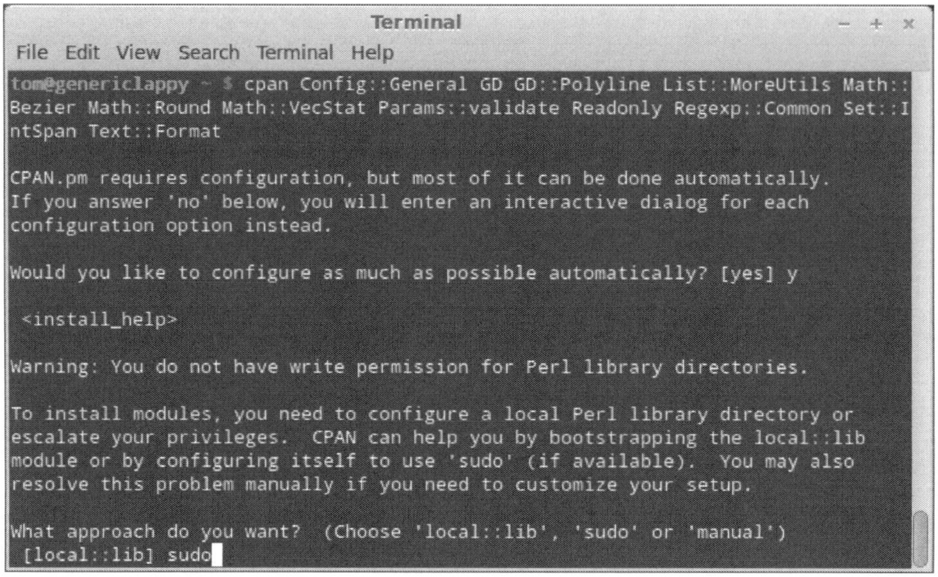

Running an example

Let's check to make sure our installation of Circos and Perl were done correctly by compiling an example image. In the Terminal window, type the following commands:

```
cd ~/

perl "Circos/bin/circos" -conf "Circos/example/etc/circos.conf"
```

After a brief pause, several dozen lines of text will scroll down the Command Prompt as various elements are "drawn" for the image. If anything is incorrect, you will see a noticeable error appear in the Terminal window. Otherwise, you will see a summary of the time elapsed to make the image.

Use your computer's file manager to navigate to `~\Circos\example` and open `circos.png` to view the successful output.

Relating to the rest of this book

Linux users are usually savvy computer users needing less assistance than users of other operating systems. The remainder of this book will refer to commands in the Windows operating environment—where user ability is far more diverse.

Everything will also be relevant to the Linux user, but the syntax will be slightly different, naturally, due to differences between the Windows Command Prompt and Linux Terminal. Here are a few key items to help you, the Linux user, relate to the remainder of the book:

- In this book, opening the Windows Command Prompt is analogous to opening the Terminal
- When you see `C:\Program Files (x86)\Circos`, relate this to `~\Circos`, that is, the Windows command `cd C:\Program Files (x86)\Circos` is the same as `cd ~\Circos` in the Terminal

Perl is not installed on my Linux distribution

Perl is usually available on Linux, but if your distribution did not contain Perl or it has been deleted, it is easy to reinstall it. Open the Terminal window and type the following command:

```
curl -L http://xrl.us/installperlnix | bash
```

Perl modules not installing correctly

If your Perl module is not installing correctly, you may need to update the GD Perl module through another method besides the `cpan` command. Usually, these issues relate to an out-of-date GD Perl library. On Debian-based systems, we can update the package through the `apt-get` command. Thereafter, we can proceed with the normal installation through `cpan`. To install, type the following commands into the terminal:

```
sudo apt-get install libgd-gd2-perl
```

```
cpan config::General GD::Polyline List::MoreUtils Math::Bezier
Math::Round Math::VecStat Params::Validate
```

Fedora and Red Hat users can install the GD Perl module with the following command:

```
yum install php-gd
```

Creating the first Circos diagram (Must know)

In this recipe, we will create a very basic Circos diagram containing links (ribbons) showing the relationship between hair and eye color. Throughout this task, we will become acquainted with Circos' genome-based terminology. As Circos' roots are in biology, the program does not read the typical tables most users are accustomed to.

Getting ready

Let's start with the simple task of graphing a relationship between a student's eye and hair color. We can expect some results: brown eyes are more common for students with brown or black hair, and blue eyes are more common amongst blondes. Circos is able to show these relationships with more clarity than a traditional table. We will be using the hair and eye color data available in the book's supplemental materials (`HairEyeColor.csv`). The data contains the information about hair and eye color of University of Delaware students.

> **Downloading the example code**
>
> You can download the example code files for all Packt books you have purchased from your account at `http://www.packtpub.com`. If you purchased this book elsewhere, you can visit `http://www.packtpub.com/support` and register to have the files e-mailed directly to you.

Create a folder `C:\Users\user_name\Circos Book\HairEyeColor`, and place the data file into the location. Here, `user_name` denotes the user name that is used to log in to your computer.

The original data is in a size that can be typically stored in a data set. Each line represents a student and their respective hair (black, brown, blonde, or red) and eye (blue, brown, green, or hazel) color. The following table shows the first 10 lines of data:

Hair	Eye
Brown	Brown
Red	Brown
Blonde	Blue
Brown	Hazel
Blonde	Blue
Brown	Blue
Black	Brown
Brown	Brown
Brown	Hazel

Before we start creating the specific diagram, let's prepare the data into a table. If you wish, you can use Microsoft Excel's PivotTable or Data Pilots of OpenOffice to transform it into a table as follows:

	Blue	Brown	Green	Hazel
Black	20	68	5	15
Blonde	94	7	15	11

	Blue	Brown	Green	Hazel
Brown	84	119	29	54
Red	17	26	14	14

In order to use the data for Circos, we need a simpler format. Open a text file and create a table only separated by spaces. We will also change the row and column titles to make it clearer, as follows:

```
X Blue_Eyes Brown_Eyes Green_Eyes Hazel_Eyes
Black_Hair 20 68 5 15
Blonde_Hair 94 7 15 11
Brown_Hair 84 119 29 54
Red_Hair 17 26 14 14
```

The `X` is simply a place holder. Save this file as `HairEyeColorTable.txt` as we are ready to use Circos.

> You can skip the process of making the raw tables. We will be using the `HairEyeColorTable.txt` file to create the Circos diagram.

How to do it...

1. Open the Command Prompt and change the directory to the location of the tableviewer tools in the `Circos\Circos Tools\tools\tableviewer\bin`, as follows:

    ```
    cd C:\Program Files (x86)\Circos\Circos Tools\tools\tableviewer\bin
    ```

2. Parse the text table (`HairEyeColorTable.txt`). This will create a new file, `HairEyeColorTable-parsed.txt`, which will be refined into a Circos diagram as follows:

    ```
    perl parse-table -file "C:\Users\user_name\Circos Book\
    HairEyeColor\HairEyeColorTable.txt" > "C:\Users\user_name\Circos
    Book\HairEyeColor\HairEyeColorTable-parsed.txt"
    ```

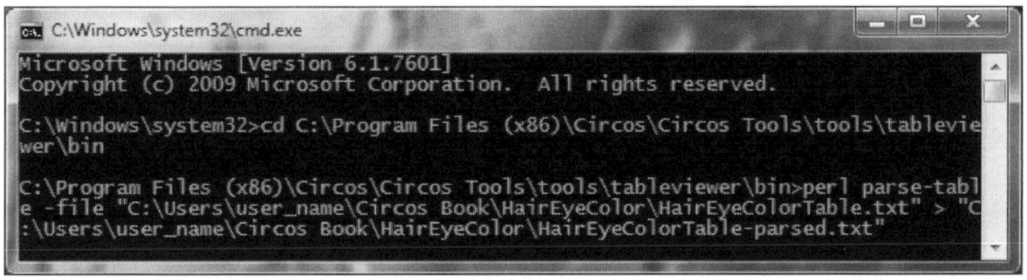

3. The parse command consists of a few parts. First, Perl's parse-table instructs Perl to execute the parse program on the `HairEyeColorTable.txt` file. Second, the **>** symbol instructs Windows to write the output into another text file called `HairEyeColorTable-parsed.txt`.

> **Linux Users**
>
> Linux users can use a simpler, shorter syntax. Steps 2 and 3 can be completed with this command:
>
> ```
> cat "~/Documents/Circos Book/HairEyeColor/
> HairEyeColorTable.txt" | bin/parse-table | bin/
> make-conf -dir "~/Documents/user_name/Circos Book/
> HairEyeColor/HairEyeColorTable-parsed.txt
> ```

Create the configuration files from the parsed table using the following command:

```
type "C:\Users\user_name\Circos Book\HairEyeColor\
HairEyeColorTable-parsed.txt" | perl make-conf -dir "C:\Users\
user_name\Circos Book\HairEyeColor\"
```

This will create 11 new configuration files. These files contain the data and style information which is needed to create the final diagram.

> This command consists of two parts. We are instructing Windows to pass the text in the `HairEyeColorTable-parsed.txt` file to the `make-conf` command. The | (pipe) character separates what we want passed along and the actual command. After the pipe, we are instructing Perl to execute the `make-conf` command and store the output into a new directory.

4. We need to create a final file, which compiles all the information. This file will also tell Circos how the diagram should appear, such as size, labels, image style, and where the diagram will be saved. We will save the diagram as `HairEyeColor.conf`.

   - The `make-conf` command gave us the `color.conf` file, which associates colors with the final diagram. In addition, the Circos installation provides us with some other basic colors and fonts. The first several lines of code are:

     ```
     <colors>
     <<include colors.conf>>
     <<include C:\Program Files (x86)\Circos\etc\colors.conf>>
     </colors>
     <fonts>
     <<include C:\Program Files (x86)\Circos\etc\fonts.conf>>
     </fonts>
     ```

- The next segment is the ideogram. These are the parameters that set the details of the image. This first set of lines specifies the spacing, color, and size of the chromosomes:

```
<ideogram>
<spacing>
default=0.01r
break=200u
</spacing>
thickness = 100p
stroke_thickness = 2
stroke_color = black
fill = yes
fill_color = black
radius = 0.7r
show_label = yes
label_font  = condensedbold
label_radius = dim(ideogram,radius) + 0.05r
label_size = 48
band_stroke_thickness = 2
show_bands = yes
fill_bands = yes
</ideogram>
```

- Next, we will define the image, including where it is stored (this location is mentioned in the following code snippet as `dir`), the file name, whether we want an SVG or PNG file, size, background color, and any rotation:

```
dir = C:\Users\user_name\Circos Book\HairEyeColor\
file = HairEyeColor
svg = yes
png = yes
24bit = yes
radius = 800p
background = white
angle_offset = +90
```

- Lastly, we will input the data and define how the links (ribbons) should look:

```
chromosomes_units = 1
karyotype = karyotype.txt
<links>
z = 0
radius = 1r - 150p
bezier_radius = 0.2r
<link cell_>
ribbon = yes
```

```
flat = yes
show = yes
color = black
thickness = 2
file = cells.txt
</link>
show_bands = yes
<<include C:\Program Files (x86)\Circos\etc\housekeeping.conf>>
```

Save this file as `HairEyeColor.conf` with the other configuration files. Have a look at the next diagram which explains all this procedure:

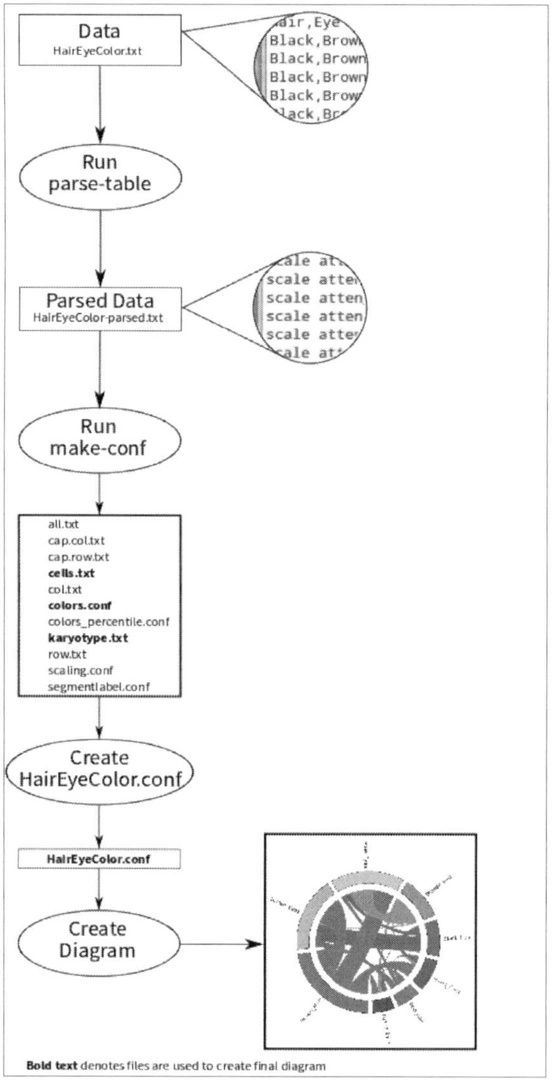

> The `make-conf` command outputs a few very important files. First, `karyotype.txt` defines each ideogram band's name, width, and color. Meanwhile, `cells.txt` is the `segdup` file containing the actual data. It is very different from our original table, but it dictates the width of each ribbon. Circos links the `karyotype` and `segdup` files to create the image. The other configuration files are mostly to set the aesthetics, placement, and size of the diagram.

5. Return to the Command Prompt and execute the following command:

```
cd C:\Users\user_name\Circos Book\HairEyeColor
perl "C:\Program Files (x86)\Circos\bin\circos" -conf
HairEyeColor.conf
```

Several lines of text will scroll across the screen. At the conclusion, `HairEyeColor.png` and `HairEyeColor.svg` will appear in the folder as shown in the next diagram:

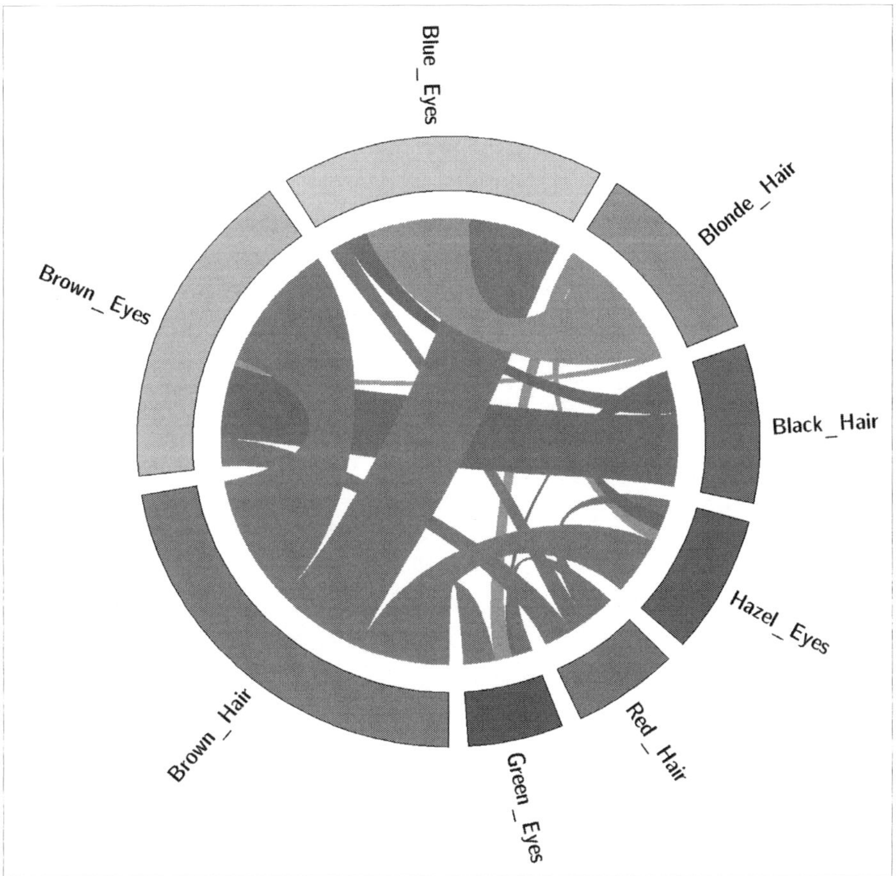

There's more...

Now we can work toward improving the quality of the image. Later, we will increase the complexity. This section will add two tweaks. First, we will change the colors so the hair and eye color will correspond to image colors—a natural way to display such data. Secondly, we will include some transparency so we can see the overlapping ribbons even better.

1. We can change the color of the ribbons by adjusting the `colors.conf` file generated by the `make-conf` command. Open the file and change the colors to:

   ```
   colorgreen_eyes = 46,139,87
   colorblack_hair = 0,0,0
   colorblue_eyes = 0,191,255
   colorbrown_hair = 205,133,63
   colorbrown_eyes = 178,34,34
   colorhazel_eyes = 208,195,131
   colorred_hair = 255,0,0
   colorblonde_hair = 242,218,145
   ```

2. Let's also add some transparency. Transparency values range from 0 (opaque) to 1 (transparent). Modify the existing colors to:

   ```
   colorgreen_eyes = 46,139,87,.2
   colorblack_hair = 0,0,0,.2
   colorblue_eyes = 0,191,255,.2
   colorbrown_hair = 205,133,63,.2
   colorbrown_eyes = 178,34,34,.2
   colorhazel_eyes = 208,195,131,.2
   colorred_hair = 255,0,0,.2
   colorblonde_hair = 242,218,145,.2
   ```

3. Save the file as `colors-new.conf`. Meanwhile, return to `HairEyeColor.conf` and change `<<include colors.conf>>` to `<<include colors-new.conf>>`.
4. Regenerate the image by using the following command:

   ```
   perl "C:/Program Files (x86)/Circos/bin/circos" -conf
   HairEyeColor.conf
   ```

This will generate the following diagram:

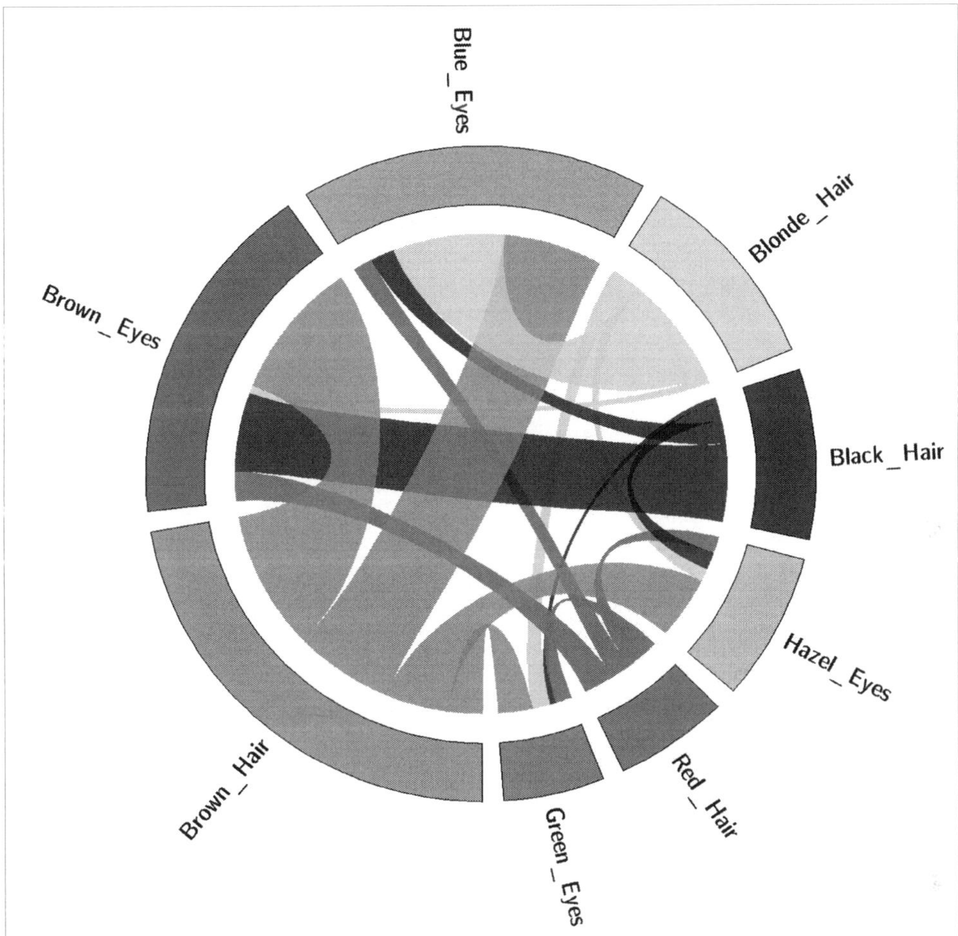

Links without ribbons

Perhaps we will find it more pertinent to show whether there is a relationship, as opposed to the quantity of a relationship. We can easily change from ribbons—whose width corresponds to the data—to simple links.

In the `HairEyeColor.conf` file, edit the `ribbon = yes` line to `ribbon = no`. Regenerate the image; the result will now be:

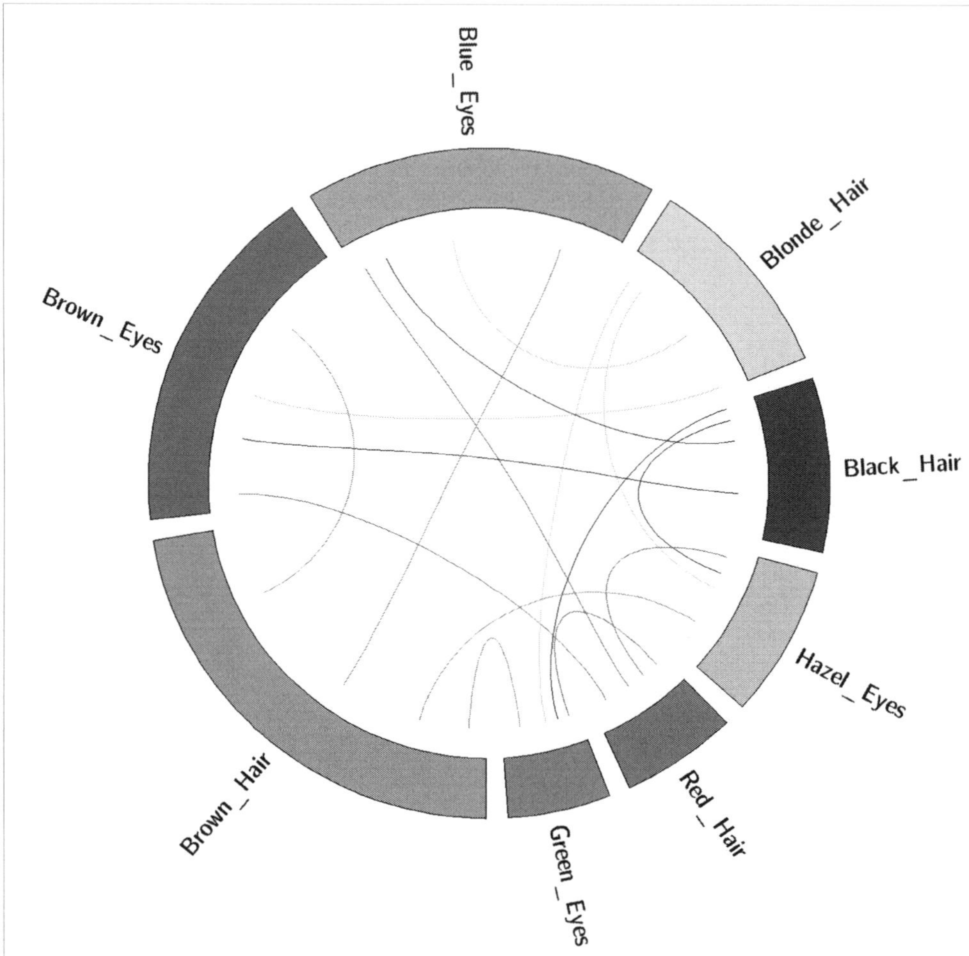

Editing the image for a final product

We may want to edit the image for a final product. For instance, Circos does not support spaces in labels, leaving an underscore for denoting a space in a diagram. This may be unacceptable for the final product. You may want to explore **Scalar Vector Graphic** (**SVG**) output. SVG is a particular format, which allows you to change image sizes with no distortion.

You can open an SVG in programs such as Adobe Illustrator (`http://www.adobe.com/products/illustrator.html`) or Inkscape (`http://inkscape.org/`) to modify the design or create a poster. SVG allows you to even select and change specific parts of the diagram.

Customizing Circos layout (Should know)

The default layout for Circos provides a nice, but chunky and sometimes inelegant diagram. However, we have the ability to customize the image output in a number of ways. In this section, we will adjust several of the image parameters to improve the output. Specifically, we will reorder the chromosomes according to their geographical area, visually combine the political parties, adjust the label sizes, add tick marks to provide a quantitative guide, and adjust the position of the labels.

Getting ready

We will introduce and use contributions to Federal elections from 2011 through summer 2012. Our goal will be to map the amount of contributions from each state to the Democratic, Republican, Libertarian, or unaffiliated political parties. Each political party, state, and American territory will form a chromosome.

Geographical data is usually, and justifiably, displayed using a map. The following diagram shows an excellent example of political contributions in the United States. Yet, sometimes maps put too much emphasis on the geography and less on specific relationships between a state and donations.

Image by Mike Tahani: `http://datahacker.tumblr.com/`

In this recipe, we will use Circos to visualize similar data as the first map. Each chromosome will represent a political party, state, or American territory. We will begin by mapping the amount of money donated to political parties by each state or territory. Instead of relying on the default settings, we will change various aesthetic aspects of the diagram.

Below is part of the original table we will use for this chapter. You can find the tabular data in `FederalContributions.txt`.

X	D	I	L	R	U
AK	684387	98950	1000	483105	500
AL	1854546	1250	6000	6286579	3000
AR	1609713	3425	950	3501270	1000
AS	2200	0	0	0	0
AZ	4276102	18290	16911	10906022	6667

How to do it...

1. Start drawing the diagram with the Democrat chromosome, followed by Republican, Independent, Libertarian, and unaffiliated political donations. We will also group each state by their geographic region. Insert the following line below the `chromosome_units` parameter:

```
chromosome_order = ^,D,R,I,L,U,|,ME,NH,VT,MA,CT,RI,|,NY,PA,PA,NJ|M
D,DE,DC,|VA,NC,SC,GA,FL,|,WV,KY,TN,AL,MS,|,AR,OK,TX,LA,|,MN,ND,SD,
NE,KS,IA,MO,|,WI,MI,IL,IN,OH,|,MT,ID,WY,NV,UT,CO,AZ,NM,|,WA,OR,CA,
|,AK,HI,GU,AS,VI
```

See the intermediate output in in the next diagram:

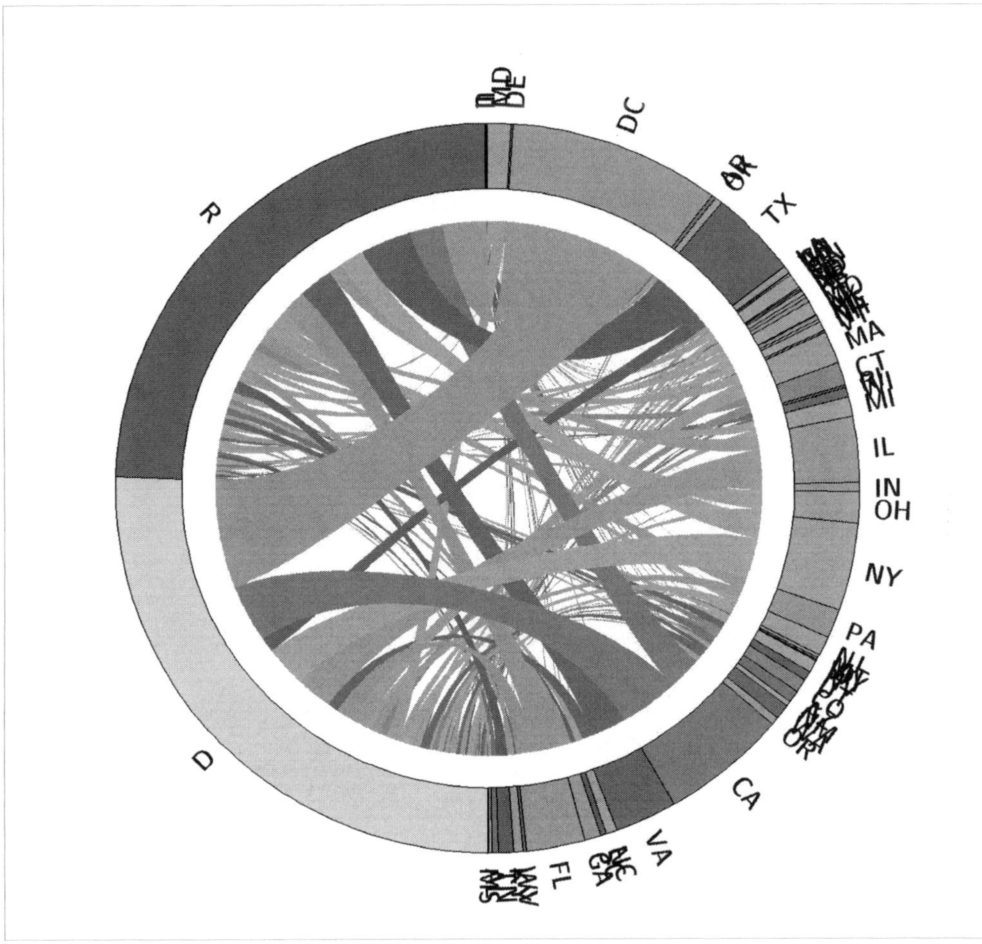

2. The chromosome length communicates crucial data points, but the width is purely aesthetic. Reduce the width as follows:

    - thickness = 25p

   This parameter specifies the thickness of the lines around the ribbon.

    - radius = 1r – 50p

   This creates a 50p (pixel) space between ribbons and the chromosome bases.

3. The smaller chromosomes make the labels for state, territory, and political party out of proportion. Reduce the font size by changing `label_size` as follows:

    - label_size = 14

See the intermediate, cumulative output in the next diagram:

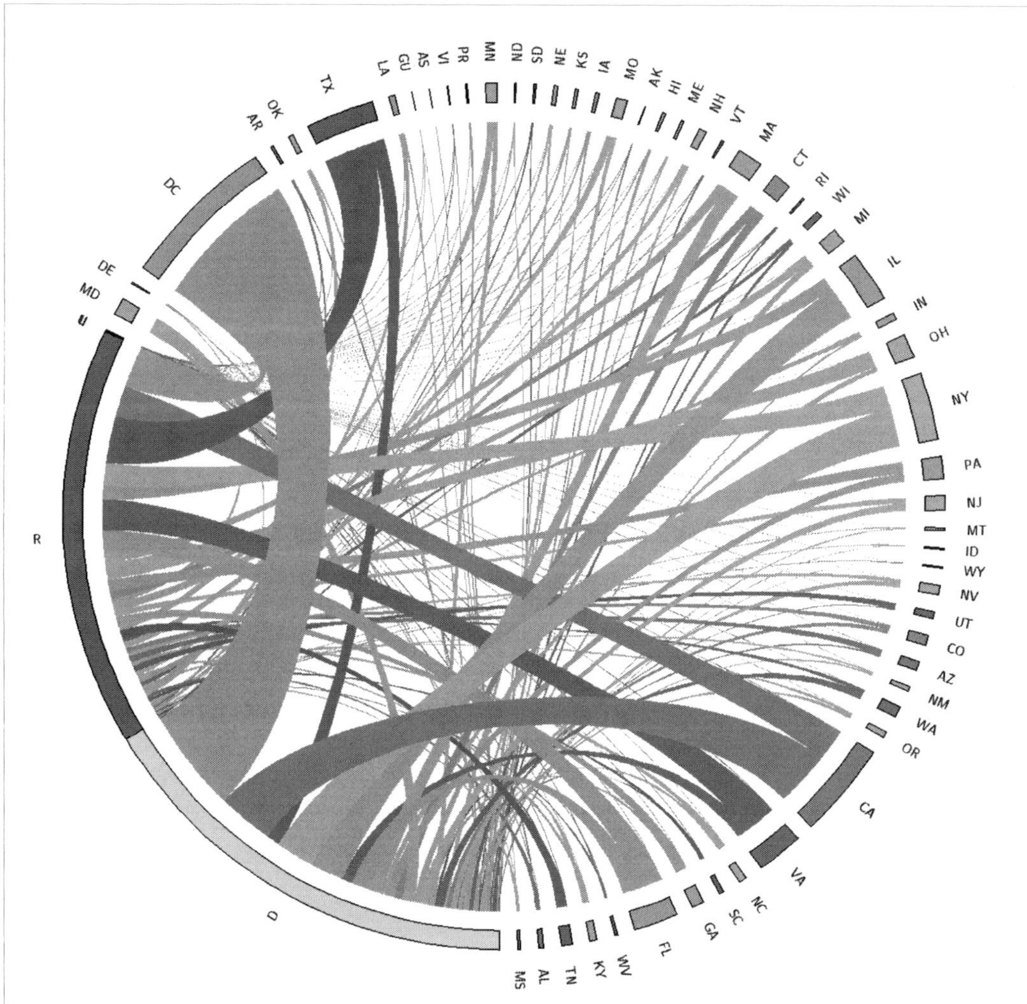

4. Now, begin the process of creating tick marks. Specifically, create an unlabeled tick mark for every $10,000,000 in donations and a labeled mark for every $50,000,000. First, create a new text file called `ticks.conf`.

5. After creating the file, insert some basic information as follows:

```
show_ticks = yes
show_tick_labels = yes
```

Thus, you can turn off tick marks or labels by adjusting a line of text instead of changing the entire file.

6. Now, let's begin defining our ticks, in particular the position, orientation, and units. Each tick will be drawn on the outside perimeter of the ideogram and the labels will face outward. Use the following code:

```
<ticks>
dims(ideogram,radius_outer)
Orientation = out
label_multiplier = 1
chromosome_display_default = yes
```

7. We need to define two types of tick marks. The first will occur at each multiple of $10,000,000 in contributions, but without any label. In our `ticks.conf` file, add this to the prior set of code:

```
<tick>
spacing = 10000000u
size = 3p
thickness = 2p
color = dgrey
show_label = no
format = %d
<tick>
```

8. Next, define the second set of ticks. These marks will occur at each multiple of $50,000,000 in donations, with a corresponding label showing a dollar sign. Continuing on the same file, type the following code:

```
<tick>
spacing = 50000000u
size = 5p
thickness = 2p
color = dgrey
show_label = yes
label_size = 7p
label_offset = 0p
format = %d
prefix = $
</tick>
```

9. Finalize the `ticks.conf` file as follows:

```
</ticks>
```

10. Return to the `FederalContributions.conf` file and insert the following line above the `<ideogram>` tag:

    ```
    <<include ticks.conf>>
    ```

    The cumulative outcome is seen in the following diagram:

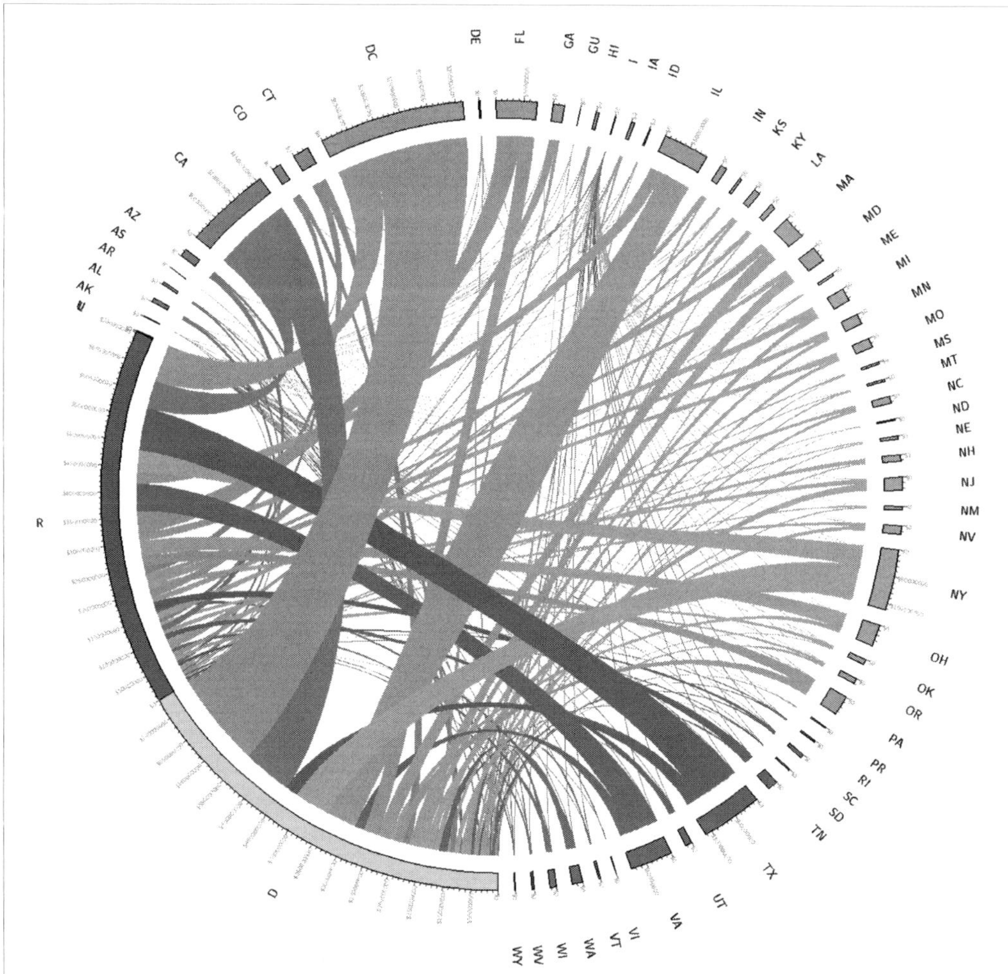

> The labels for tick marks will interfere with labels for political parties, states, and territories. We can adjust the labels in the `ElectionContributions.conf` file with: `label_radius = dims(ideogram,radius) + 0.15r`. Previously, the labels were set at `0.05r`.

11. Compile the final diagram by opening the Command Prompt and typing the following code:

```
perl "C:\Program Files (x86)\Circos\bin\circos -conf "C:\Users\
user_name\Circos Book\FederalContributions\FederalContributions-
final.conf"
```

There's more...

Circos has a high **data-to-ink** (or **data-to-pixel**) ratio, which means almost all of the space on the screen is used to communicate data. Yet Circos diagrams can hold overwhelming amounts of information. A way to simplify comparisons is to facet the data; that is, filter the graph to specific components and display each graph separately. In this case we can create two graphs, one showing only Democratic contributions and the other showing only Republican contributions, by filtering data.

Fortunately, we do not need to edit the actual data; instead, we are able to filter by using parameters in the Circos configuration files. We will use both these methods, one for the Democrat data and the other for Republican.

1. Let's start with Democrat contributions. Open the `FederalContributions.conf` file and insert the following line of code, which instructs Circos about the political parties not to include:

   ```
   chromosomes = -R;-L;-U
   ```

   This excludes the Republican, Libertarian, and other political parties.

   ```
   chromosomes_display_default = yes
   ```

2. Save the file as `FederalContributions-democrat.conf`.
3. Generate the diagram with the following lines of code:

   ```
   cd "C:\Users\user_name\Circos Book\FederalContributions"
   perl "C:\Program Files (x86)\Circos\bin\circos" -conf
   FederalContributions-democrats.conf
   perl "C:\Program Files (x86)\Circos\bin\circos" -conf
   FederalContributions-republicans.conf
   ```

You can view the output in the following figure:

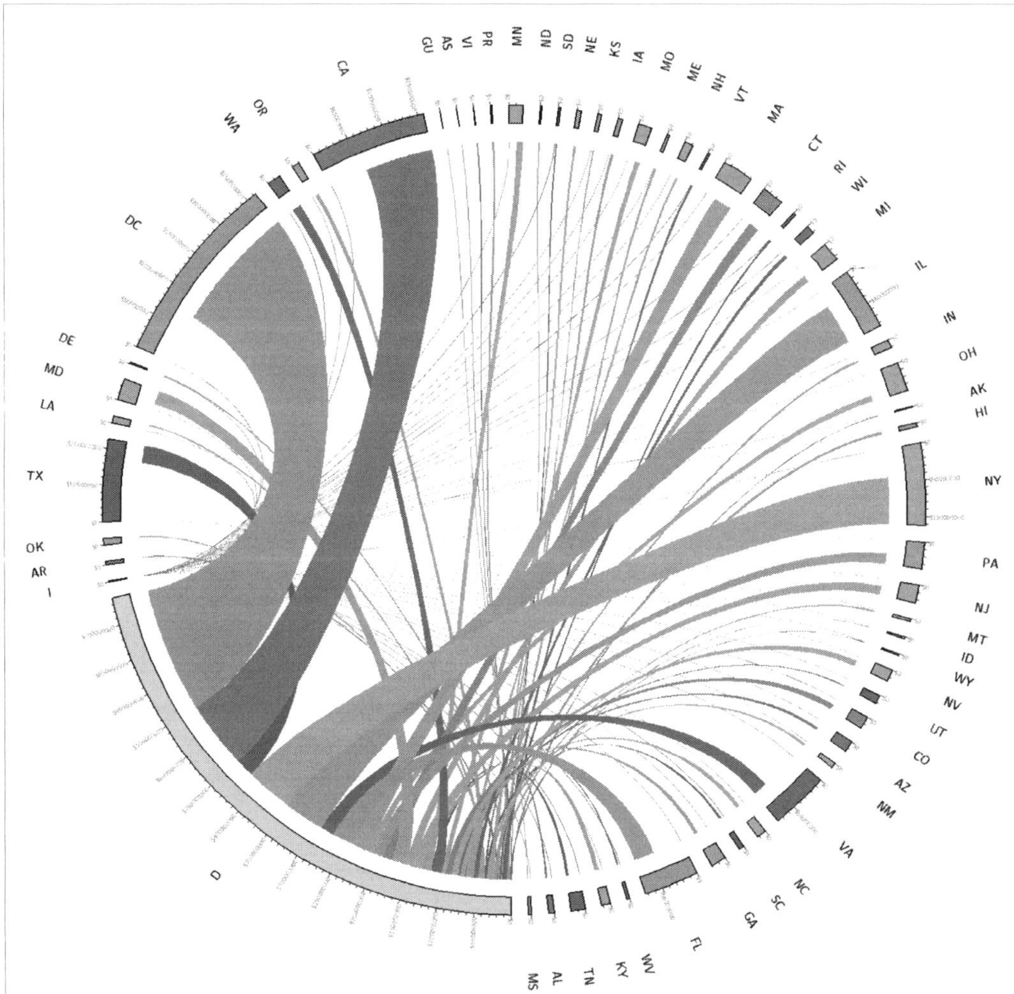

Formatting links with rules (Become an expert)

Our previous example showed the relationship between donations for each state and territory with political parties. The analysis was shown at the state and territory level, but within each ribbon, there were hundreds or even thousands of individual donations. Are these donations from thousands of different individuals or are there a few donors who comprise most of the amounts given? In this recipe, we will analyze data at the individual levels to visualize any big donors.

With this strategy, we can use additional techniques to help illuminate the data. We will **bundle** smaller donations into a single ribbon to improve visibility and we will use **rules** to visually highlight donations of at least $100,000.

Getting ready

This recipe uses a similar, but new, data set linking each individual donation within a state to a political party. Each chromosome will denote a party, state, or territory, but each link or ribbon will denote a particular donation as shown in the following diagram:

Although the diagram looks similar, it is much larger than our previous set of data. To illustrate, let's examine the first and last eight rows of the data set in `Circos Book\3 - Customizing Circos Layout\FederalIndividualContributions\cells.txt`.

The next table provides the data set of first eight rows:

1	link000001	AK	1	700	color=colorak
2	link000001	D	1	700	color=colorak
3	link000002	AK	701	5701	color=colorak
4	link000002	I	1	5000	color=colorak
5	link000003	AK	5702	10702	color=colorak
6	link000003	I	5001	10000	color=colorak
7	link000004	AK	10703	15703	color=colorak
8	link000004	I	10001	15000	color=colorak

The last eight rows are shown in the next table:

880051	link440027	WY	1885083	1948983	color=colorwy
880052	link440027	R	7.03E+08	7.03E+08	color=colorwy
880053	link440028	WY	1948984	2029784	color=colorwy
880054	link440028	R	7.03E+08	7.03E+08	color=colorwy
880055	link440029	WY	2029785	2031285	color=colorwy
880056	link440029	D	7.38E+08	7.38E+08	color=colorwy
880057	link440030	WY	2031286	2031786	color=colorwy
880058	link440030	R	7.03E+08	7.03E+08	color=colorwy
880059	link440027	WY	1885083	1948983	color=colorwy
880060	link440027	R	7.03E+08	7.03E+08	color=colorwy

Each line represents individual contributions. As the table shows, there are 880,060 rows of data representing 440,030 contributions.

Consequently, the diagram takes much longer to compile. This diagram compiled in 36 minutes, whereas previous diagrams only took around one minute. You can compile the previous diagram in Terminal as well:

```
cd C:\User\user_name\Circos Book\3 - Customizing Circos Layout\
FederalIndividualContributions\
```

```
perl "C:\Program Files (x86)\Circos\bin\circos" -conf
FederalIndividualContributions.conf -debug_group timer
```

This instance will generate the images and a summary of the elapsed time. Circos also includes the ability to provide other logs to help you diagnose issues. To learn more, see the *Debugging output options* recipe coming ahead.

> To save time, you can run the first 30,000 links by inserting the following command into the `FederalIndividualContributions.conf` under the `<link segdup>` tag:
>
> `record_limit = 30000`

Now, we will turn our attention to bundling links and using rules to highlight large donations.

How to do it...

1. Let's create several layers of links where smaller donations become more transparent and donations over $1,000,000 are fully visible. Within the `<link>` tag, enter the following rules:

```
<rules>
  <rule>
    importance = 100
    condition = max(_SIZE1_,_SIZE2_) < 1000000
    color = eval(_color_."_a1")
  </rule>
  <rule>
    importance = 90
    condition = max(_SIZE1_,_SIZE2_) < 500000
    color = eval(_color_."_a2")
  </rule>
  <rule>
    importance = 80
    condition = max(_SIZE1_,_SIZE2_) < 250000
    color = eval(_color_."_a3")
  </rule>
  <rule>
    importance = 70
    condition = max(_SIZE1_,_SIZE2_) < 100000
    color = eval(_color_."_a4")
  </rule>
  <rule>
    importance = 60
    condition = max(_SIZE1_,_SIZE2_) < 50000
```

```
    color = eval(_color_."_a5")
  </rule>
  <rule>
    importance = 50
    condition = max(_SIZE1_,_SIZE2_) < 25000
    color = eval(_color_."_a6")
  </rule>
  <rule>
    importance = 40
    condition = max(_SIZE1_,_SIZE2_) < 10000
    color = eval(_color_."_a7")
  </rule>
  <rule>
    importance = 30
    condition = max(_SIZE1_,_SIZE2_) < 5000
    color = eval(_color_."_a8")
  </rule>
  <rule>
    importance = 20
    condition = max(_SIZE1_,_SIZE2_) < 1000
    color = eval(_color_."_a9")
  </rule>
  <rule>
    importance = 10
    condition = max(_SIZE1_,_SIZE2_) < 500
    color = eval(_color_."_a10")
  </rule>
  <rule>
    importance = 5
    condition = max(_SIZE1_,_SIZE2_) < 100
    color = eval(_color_."_a11")
  </rule>
</rules>
```

2. Within the `<image>` tag, type the following code:

```
auto_alpha_colors = yes
auto_alpha_steps  = 11
```

Notice that `auto_alpha_steps` is equal to `11`, the same as the last rule which specified `_a11`. You can view the output of this rule in the next diagram:

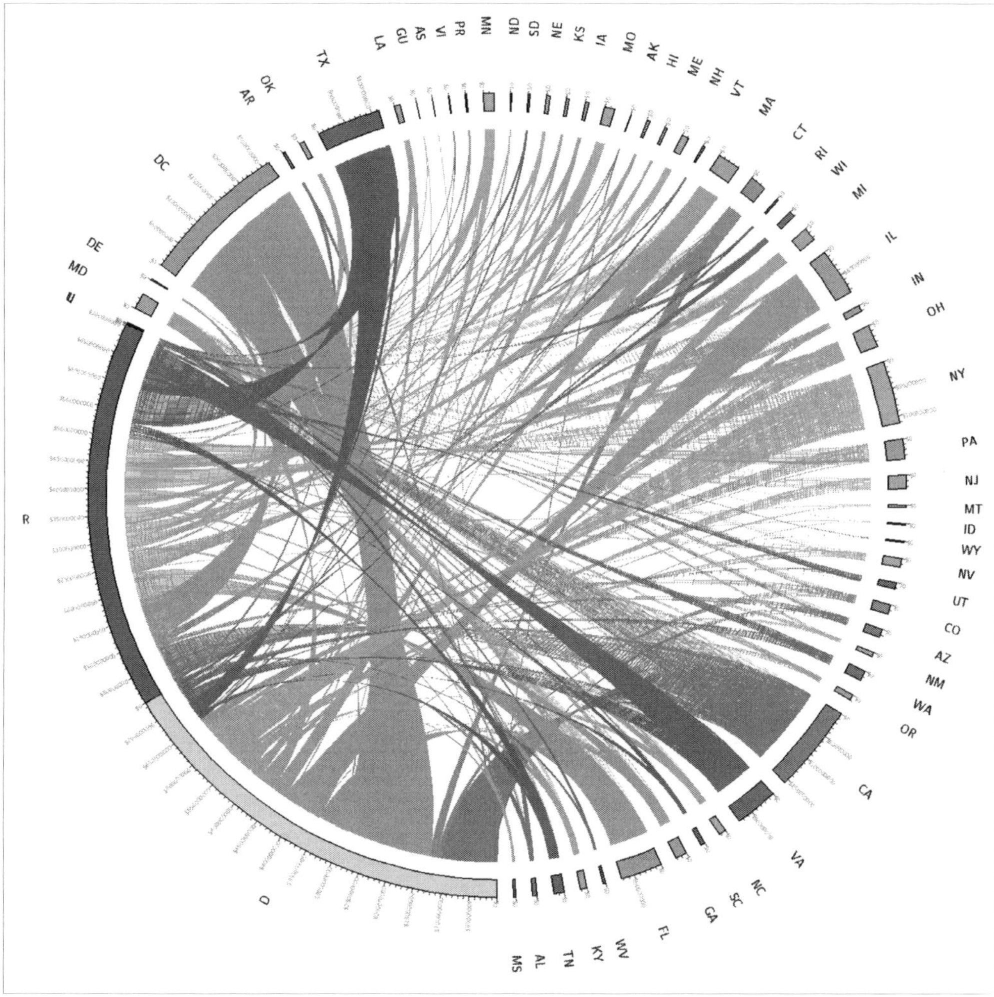

How it works...

The first step of our diagram turned `auto_alpha_colors` on with 11 steps. This enables us to easily add transparency to any colors in the `colors.conf` file, such as `red_a5`, without editing the `colors.conf` file. The smallest value, `_a0`, indicates there is no transparency, while the largest value means the least relative transparency. Using this method will never make links fully invisible, instead the transparency value is determined by N/(`auto_alpha_steps` + 1). In this instance, `red_a11` would be 11/(11+1) = 91.67 percent and `red_a5` would be 5/(11+1) = 41.67 percent transparent.

The rules we used consisted of three parts: importance, condition, and color. **Importance** merely informs Circos which rule is more important in case there are any conflicts, which is not an issue in this example.

Condition is the important criterion in this example. We instructed Circos to return the size of the link (for example, donation amount) to compare to our thresholds. Once a condition is met, the rule applies the original color with a corresponding transparency. For instance, if there is a donation from Arizona under $500 but over $100, Circos applies `coloraz_a10`.

There's more...

Rules can be used on nearly every aesthetic parameter in a Circos diagram, including applying multiple rules to each link. Using a similar syntax from the previous example, you can apply multiple rules and control other parameters using the parameters in the next couple of sections.

Applying multiple rules

This example used multiple rules, but only applied one criterion. Once a link meets a criterion, Circos stops applying other rules and advances to the next link. However, we may want to have Circos check each link against every rule—regardless if one has been met.

To enable Circos to check links against all rules even if one has been met, enter the following command below `<rules>`:

```
flow = continue
```

Remember to set the important options within the rules so Circos can prioritize conflicting instructions.

Additional rule conditions

The example used the `_SIZEn_` condition to determine the size of the link. Circos is also able to determine several other characteristics of the links and chromosomes, as follows:

- `_CHRn_`: This denotes the chromosomes connected within the links
- `_STARTn_`: This indicates the start position of the link
- `_ENDn_`: This shows the end position of the link
- `_POSITIONn_`: This is the middle position within the link
- `_SIZEn_`: This indicates the size of the span for the link
- `_INTERCHR_`: This has a binary value of 1 if the link is connected to another chromosome
- `_INTRACHR_`: This has a binary value of 1 if the link is connected to the originating chromosome

In this data set, each link is connected to another chromosome. Thus, any rule invoking `_INTERCHR_` will always be true, while any rule invoking `_INTRACHR_` will always be false.

Meanwhile, we can format the link in other ways besides color. For instance, we can place any contribution to Democrats at the top of the diagram using the `z` (depth) parameter as follows:

```
<rules>
<rule>
importance = 100
condition = (_CHR2_ eq "D")
z = 80
</rule>
<rule>
importance = 50
condition = (_CHR2_ eq "R")
z = 40
</rule>
</rules>
```

Here is a list of several ways to format links through rules:

- `Color`: This represents the color of the link.
- `Z`: This is the **depth** of the link; a higher value indicates the relative priority of being placed on top.
- `Thickness`: This is the thickness of the link.
- `Radius`: This is the length of the link from the ideogram's center to the beginning of the link. It can be used to control the space between chromosomes and the beginning of links.
- `bezier_radius`: This controls the "curviness" of each link. The value `0r` represents flat links while `1r` indicates circular links.

Reducing links with bundlelinks tool (Become an expert)

Large diagrams, such as the federal contributions dataset, are rich with data but may overwhelm the reader. Circos includes a tool to bundle links within a user-defined range. In this recipe, we will use the `bundlelinks` tool to combine small links no greater than $1,000 into groups of at least five.

How to do it...

1. We will use the data associated with `ElectionIndividualContributions.conf`. In the Terminal window, type the following commands:

   ```
   cd C:\User\user_name\Circos Book\ElectionIndividualContributions\
   ```

   ```
   perl "C:\Program Files (x86)\Circos\Circos Tools\tools\bundlelinks\bin\bundlelinks" -links cells.txt -max_gap_1 1000 -min_bundle_membership 5 > cells_bundled.txt
   ```

2. Open the `colors.conf` file and add a new color as follows:

   ```
   chr = 0,0,0,100
   ```

3. Open `ElectionIndividualContributions.conf` and note the change highlighted in the `<link>` tag, as follows:

   ```
   <link cell_>
     ribbon       = yes
     flat         = yes
     show         = yes
     thickness    = 2
     file         = cells_bundled.txt
   </link>
   ```

4. Generate the new diagram with the following command:

   ```
   perl "C:\Program Files (x86)\Circos\bin\circos" -conf ElectionIndividualContributions-rules-bundled.conf
   ```

The output is visible in the following diagram:

How it works...

Circos' `bundlelinks` tool evaluates the dataset we prepared for the diagram. Our desire was to combine small links into larger groups to reduce the number of ribbons that Circos must draw on the diagram. This helps reduce the amount of visual clutter and reduce the amount of time required to create the final diagram.

Specifically, the `bundlelinks` tool read our original data source to denote any ribbon which was less than $1,000—the amount we specified. Once it identifies small ribbons, the script combines at least five smaller ribbons into a single ribbon.

Adding data tracks – heatmap (Become an expert)

Links and ribbons are a predominant feature of Circos diagrams, but it is possible to add additional data through data tracks. So far, we have used ribbons to demonstrate political contributions to political parties. In this recipe, we will use heatmaps to show if the concentration of donations are a few or many donors.

Getting ready

In this dataset, we count the number of donors from each state who gave money to a political party. Specifically, we count the number of donors from Alaska who gave money to Democrats, the number of donors from Alaska who gave money to Republicans, and so on. Ultimately, we will be able to see if donations come from a few or many donors.

We will need to use the `heatmaps.txt` file from `C:\Users\user_name\Circos Book\`. The structure of that file is shown in the following table. The first column denotes the state or territory—we will not plot heatmaps for the political parties. The second column shows Circos where to start the heatmap and the third column shows the ending position. The difference between the second and third column is the total amount donors from each state gave to a particular party. The last column shows the number of people who gave a donation.

AK	583555	1267942	531
AK	1500	100450	50
AK	100450	583555	585

This dataset continues with all other states, and we will look into the last three rows in the next table:

WY	2750	3000	1
WY	4750	1494076	792
WY	0	2750	3

> Creating a file to work with Circos data tracks is not easy and there are no built-in tools that will always generate the appropriate files. You will need to find a way to create files for data tracks, which might include several tools, such as a spreadsheet program, a text editor, or even a programming language to create a correctly formatted file.

Data to generate heatmaps and other data tracks must follow the space-separated format of `CHR START END VALUE`, where `CHR` is the identifier which is also used in the karyotype file, `START` denotes the start position, `END` is the end position, and `VALUE` is a number Circos will use to determine the color.

How to do it...

1. First, we can enter the standard parameters and configuration files from the last recipe. Take care to note the changes to the file output and file name in this recipe.

```
<colors>
<<include colors.conf>> # colors generated from make-conf
<<include C:\Program Files (x86)\Circos\etc\colors.conf>> # pre-
installed basic colors and fonts
</colors>

<fonts>
<<include C:\Program Files (x86)\Circos\etc\fonts.conf>>
</fonts>

<<include ticks.conf>>

<ideogram>

<spacing>
  default = 0.01r
    <pairwise R>
      spacing = 0u
    </pairwise>
    <pairwise L>
      spacing = 0u
    </pairwise>
</spacing>

thickness        = 25p
stroke_thickness = 2
stroke_color     = black
fill             = yes
```

```
fill_color       = black

radius          = 0.7r
show_label      = yes  # whether labels are shown
label_font      = condensedbold  # font used for labels
label_radius    = dims(ideogram,radius) + 0.15r  # how far away the
labels appear from the chromosome bands
label_size      = 14

# cytogenetic bands
band_stroke_thickness = 2
show_bands            = yes
fill_bands            = yes
</ideogram>

<image>
dir = C:\Users\user_name\Dropbox\Circos Data Visualization Book\
Book\4 - Data tracks\data
file  = ElectionContributions-heatmap
svg = yes
png = yes
24bit = yes
radius          = 800p
background      = white
angle_offset    = +90
</image>

chromosomes_units             = 1
chromosomes_order   = ^,D,R,L,U
karyotype    = karyotype.txt
```

2. Now, we can include the beginning of the `<plots>` parameter, where we specify the type of plot (heatmap), the list of colors we want to include (a series of nine shades of grey color), and the color and border of each heatmap. Use the following code:

```
# include heatmap files
<plots>
color = greys-9-seq
stroke_thickness = 1
stroke_color = white
```

3. After specifying the plot type, we can include the specific heatmap data (`heatmap.txt`) and the position on the diagram:

```
<plot>
type = heatmap
file = heatmap.txt
```

```
r0 = 0.95r
r1 = 0.95r + 25p
</plot>
</plots>
```

4. Conclude the file by including the segdup file with the links and the housekeeping information, as follows:

```
<links>

z      = 0
# Adjust the radius to control how far away a ribbon/link appears
from the chromosomes.
radius = 1r - 50p
bezier_radius = 0.2r
bezier_radius_purity = 0.6

<link cell_>
ribbon        = yes
flat          = yes
show          = yes
color         = black
thickness     = 2
file          = cells.txt
</link>

</links>

show_bands              = yes

# The housekeeping.conf file is required, includes some basic
parameters.
<<include C:\Program Files (x86)\Circos\etc\housekeeping.conf>>
```

5. Finally, save the file as `ElectionContributions-heatmap.conf` in the same directory as the other configuration files and generate the diagram by opening the Command Prompt and entering the following commands:

```
cd C:\Users\user_name\Circos Book\

perl "C:\Program Files (x86)\Circos\bin\circos" -conf
ElectionContributions-heatmap.conf
```

The final output is shown in the following diagram:

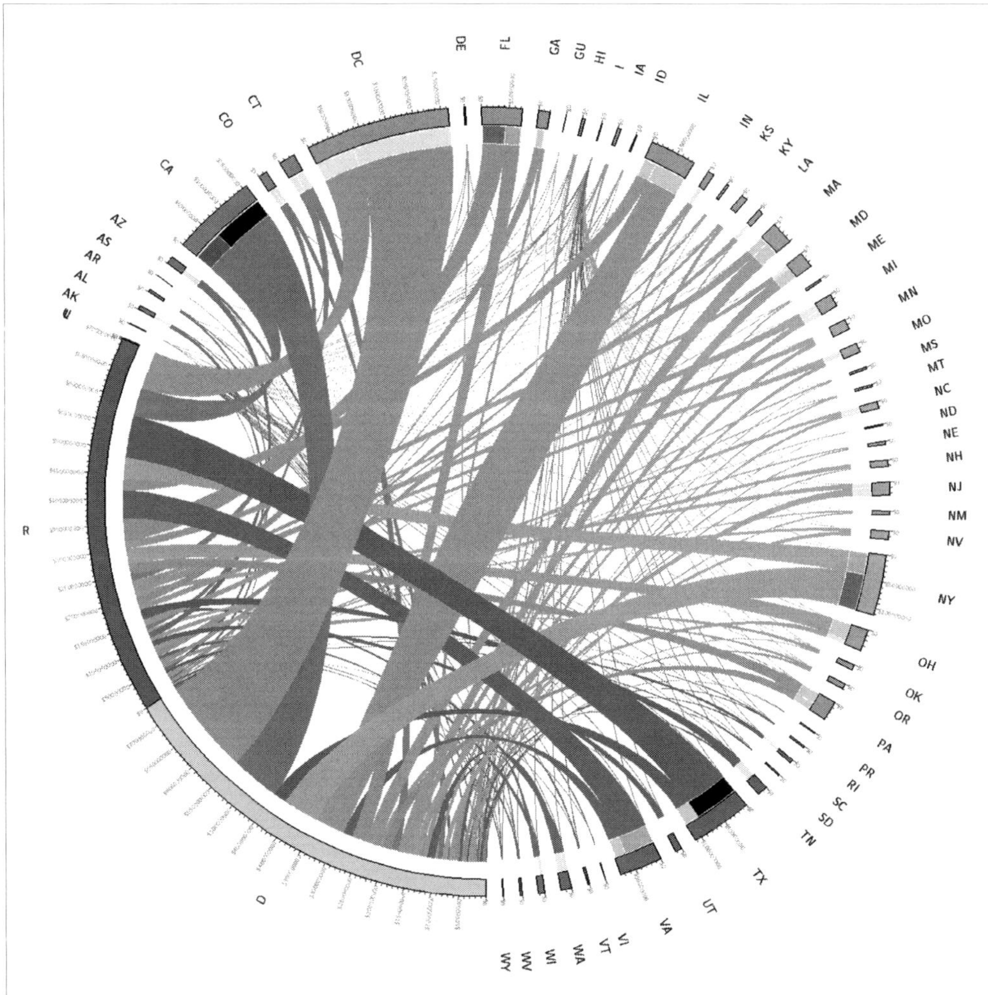

How it works...

The process is similar to prior diagrams, but the two additions are the `heatmap.txt` file and the `<plots>` parameter.

The `<plots>` parameter makes Circos ready for a new type of plot besides links and ribbons. Here we can define the type of plot and the color of the borders. Within this parameter, we may choose to plot one or more data tracks. Once we reference the data, we must determine the positioning. In this example, we chose to start the heatmaps at 95 percent of the diagrams' radius. The top portions of the heatmaps are higher by 25 pixels than the base regions.

> **Position of heatmaps and ribbons**
>
> Recall that the starting point of the links and ribbons are set by the radius parameter in the `<links>` segment. If the data tracks (for example, heatmaps) and ribbons overlap, you can adjust the radius parameter in addition to `r0` and `r1` in the `<plot>` section to fix any issues.

We gave Circos nine shades of grey to label each cell. Each color can be referenced by an index number—one through nine. Circos chooses the color to assign with the following formula:

*color_index = num_colors * [(value-min)/(value-max)]*

In this example, the darker shades of grey—all the way to black—denote more individuals donating to a party. For instance, a black segment shows that many people from California donated to the Democratic Party and a similar black segment shows many people donated to the Republicans. However, Washington D.C., even though it was the largest total contributor, had relatively few donors. There are other ways to show the data (for example, average contributions per person) and we can adjust for other factors too (for example, population), but this method allows us to explore the data further.

Circos only supports labels around the diagram, it does not support a separate legend for values associated with each color.

There's more...

In this task, we chose to use a pre-defined color palette based on the popular Colorbrewer palettes. Circos includes several of the palettes, but you can also choose your own color templates. In the next section we will discuss each in greater detail.

Predefined Colorbrewer colors

Colorbrewer is a popular template for predefined colors, because here one can choose colors based on the predominant color palette, sequential or diverging colors, or on an abstract palette (for example, pastels). You can choose these in combination with the number of colors you need, between three and nine colors. Our example used a series of nine different shades of sequential grey colors, thus `greys-9-seq`.

The syntax for the color scheme follows the same pattern, specifically, color-numcolors-type. Darker colors indicate a higher value, but if you wish we can reverse the colors with `-rev`. For instance, reversing the color scheme from our earlier example would require `greys-9-seq-rev`.

The following is a list of different color codes; each can be adjusted with the number of colors and by adding reverse shading if you wish. A full listing of colors is available at `C:\Program Files (x86)\Circos\etc\brewer.all.conf`.

```
# qualitative
accent-6-qual
dark2-6-qual
paired-6-qual
pastel1-6-qual
pastel2-6-qual
set1-6-qual
set2-6-qual
set3-6-qual

# sequential
blues-6-seq
bugn-6-seq
bupu-6-seq
gnbu-6-seq
greens-6-seq
greys-6-seq
oranges-6-seq
orrd-6-seq
pubu-6-seq
pubugn-6-seq
purd-6-seq
purples-6-seq
rdpu-6-seq
reds-6-seq
ylgn-6-seq
ylgnbu-6-seq
ylorbr-6-seq
ylorrd-6-seq

# diverging
brbg-6-div
piyg-6-div
prgn-6-div
puor-6-div
rdbu-6-div
rdgy-6-div
rdylbu-6-div
rdylgn-6-div
spectral-6-div
```

Custom color codes

As always, you can list your own set of pre-defined colors. Revisiting the earlier segment of code, we can replace the colors with grey, red, green, blue, purple, orange, and yellow using the following code:

```
<plots>
type = heatmap
color = grey, red, green, blue, purple, orange, yellow
stroke_thickness = 1
stroke_color = white
  <plot>
  file = heatmap.txt
  r0 = 0.95r
  r1 = 0.95r + 25p
  </plot>
</plots>
```

This configuration will use grey to denote the smallest values and yellow to represent the largest. The output of this color scheme is shown in the following diagram:

Adding data tracks – histogram (Become an expert)

Data tracks are a powerful way to add more layers of information in a diagram. We will avoid using links and ribbons in this recipe and draw a simple histogram.

Getting ready

Election contributions can be given to presidential or congressional candidates. The `histogram.txt` file contains the corresponding data for this recipe.

The format required for the histogram follows a pattern similar to our heatmap example as `CHR START END VALUE`. The first column `CHR` is the state or territory, the second denotes the starting position of the histogram, the third specifies the ending point, and the last column is the value plotted on the diagram.

The values in this example are either 1 (for presidential contribution) or -1 (for congressional contribution).

How to do it...

1. The primary configuration file for this example will be called `ElectionContributions-histogram.conf`. Include the following standard set of parameters, noting the location and file name for the output:

```
<colors>
<<include colors.conf>> # colors generated from make-conf
<<include C:\Program Files (x86)\Circos\etc\colors.conf>> # pre-
installed basic colors and fonts
</colors>

<fonts>
<<include C:\Program Files (x86)\Circos\etc\fonts.conf>>
</fonts>

<<include ticks.conf>>

<ideogram>

<spacing>
  default = 0.01r
    <pairwise R>
      spacing = 0u
    </pairwise>
    <pairwise L>
      spacing = 0u
```

```
    </pairwise>
  </spacing>

  thickness         = 25p
  stroke_thickness = 2
  stroke_color      = black
  fill              = yes
  fill_color        = black

  radius           = 0.7r
  show_label       = yes  # whether labels are shown
  label_font       = condensedbold  # font used for labels
  label_radius     = dims(ideogram,radius) + 0.15r  # how far away the
  labels appear from the chromosome bands
  label_size       = 14

  # cytogenetic bands
  band_stroke_thickness = 2
  show_bands            = yes
  fill_bands            = yes
  </ideogram>

  <image>
  dir = C:\Users\user_name\Dropbox\Circos Data Visualization Book\
  Book\4 - Data tracks\data
  file  = ElectionContributions-histogram
  svg = yes
  png = yes
  24bit = yes
  radius           = 800p
  background       = white
  angle_offset     = +90
  </image>

  chromosomes_units             = 1
  chromosomes_order   = ^,D,R,L,U
  karyotype    = karyotype.txt
```

2. Now, include the parameters for the heatmap— the same as in the previous recipe—in this diagram. The syntax will appear slightly different, but it performs the same function:

```
# include data track files
<plots>
show = yes
  <plot>
    type = heatmap
    color = greys-9-seq
    file = heatmap.txt
    stroke_thickness = 1
```

```
    stroke_color = white
    r0 = 0.95r
    r1 = 0.95r + 25p
  </plot>
```

3. Now include the `<plot>` command for the histogram. In this graph we will limit the axis from `0` to `1`, so presidential contributions are visible and congressional contributions are suppressed:

```
<plot>
    type = histogram
    color = grey
    file = histogram.txt
    fill_color = grey
    thickness = 1
    extend_bin = yes
```

This creates histograms with contiguous bars.

```
    r0 = 0.90r
    r1 = 0.93r
    min = 0
    max = 1
  </plot>
</plots>
```

4. As we're laying a heatmap and a histogram, we need to adjust the positions of the ribbons. The following section of code is similar to prior examples, but the highlighted sections have been changed to provide space for the data tracks:

```
<links>

z       = 0
# Adjust the radius to control how far away a ribbon/link appears
from the chromosomes.
radius = 0.90r
bezier_radius = 0.2r
bezier_radius_purity = 0.6

<link cell_>
ribbon        = yes
flat          = yes
show          = yes
color         = black
thickness     = 2
file          = cells.txt
</link>

</links>
```

5. Finally, finish the file with the the necessary parameters, as follows:

```
show_bands = yes

# The housekeeping.conf file is required, includes some basic
parameters.
<<include C:\Program Files (x86)\Circos\etc\housekeeping.conf>>
```

6. Generate the diagram by opening the Command Prompt and typing the following commands:

```
cd C:\Users\user_name\Circos Book\

perl "C:\Program Files (x86)\Circos\bin\circos" -conf
ElectionContributions-histogram.conf
```

The output is shown in in the next diagram:

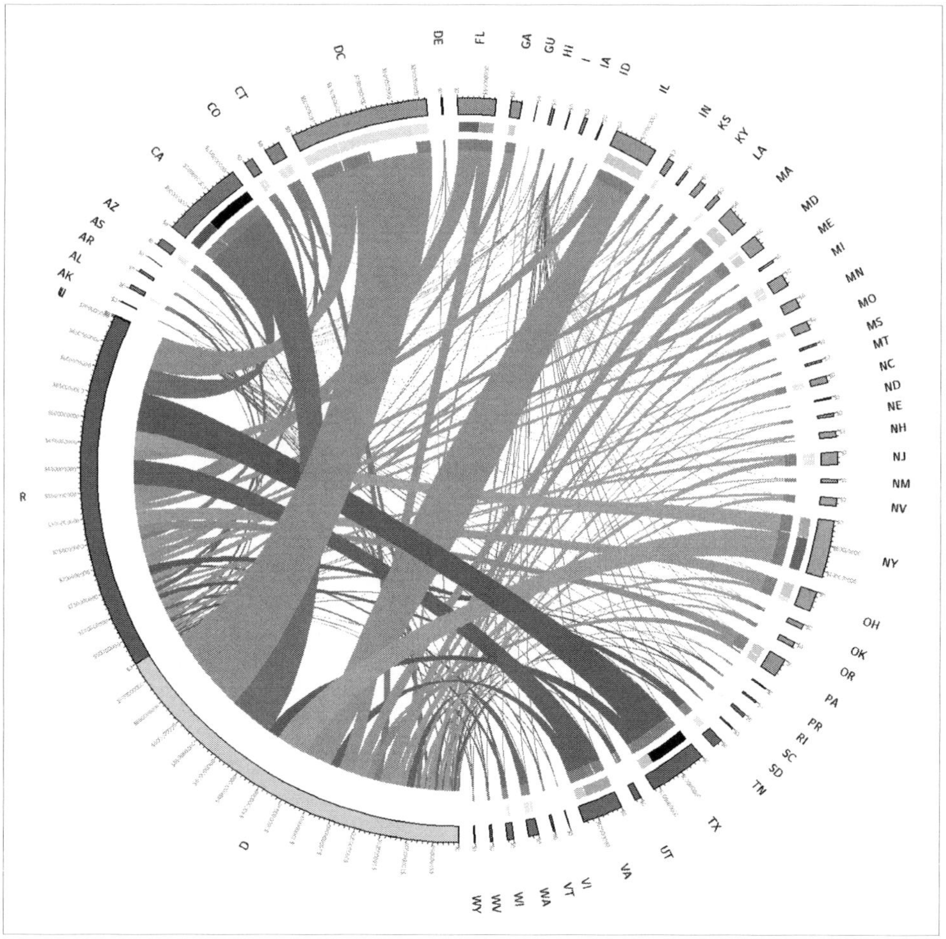

How it works...

This recipe adds another data track to our previous diagram. We are able to add the additional data tracks through multiple `<plot>` commands. We format the first set of heatmaps in the first set of the `<plot>` tag using the same parameters we used in the previous recipe.

We also created a set of histograms using another set of `<plot>` commands. The `<plot>` commands are created with several components as follows:

- The `type` command allows us to define the diagram type, such as histogram.
- The `file` parameter points Circos to the data file.
- There are several aesthetic parameters such as `color`, `fill_color`, and `thickness` that define the color and look of the histogram.
- The parameter `r0` instructs Circos where to begin to draw the innermost part of the histogram. The parameter `r1` instructs Circos where to draw the outermost part of the histogram. The difference between these two parameters gives the maximum width of the histogram.

We also defined the size of the y-axis for the data. In particular, this task plotted data between 0 and 1. However, our data ranged from either -1 to 1. As a result, our histogram had two states—a bar occupying the full width and no bar.

There's more...

Relative sizing with radius

Every aspect of a Circos diagram can be sized with pixels, but it is better to specify positioning as relative to the radius of the diagram. If we choose to alter the size, each component will move in proportion. However, we have to do some math when creating a diagram.

In the first step, we defined the radius as `800p`. The heatmaps begin at 95 percent of the radius, thus, they begin at *800p * 0.95= 760p* from the center. The point outside of the heatmap (`r1`) ends at *800 * 0.98125= 785p* from the center. The portion outside of the histogram begins at 0.93r or 744p from the center. We chose to have the ribbon and histogram contiguous, so both started at 0.90r, which was at 720p from the center. This is explained in the next diagram:

When building the diagram, some simple mathematics will help you get the right proportions. Writing the parameters in terms of radii will let it scale proportionally in the future.

[PACKT] PUBLISHING

Thank you for buying
Circos Data Visualization How-to

About Packt Publishing

Packt, pronounced 'packed', published its first book "*Mastering phpMyAdmin for Effective MySQL Management*" in April 2004 and subsequently continued to specialize in publishing highly focused books on specific technologies and solutions.

Our books and publications share the experiences of your fellow IT professionals in adapting and customizing today's systems, applications, and frameworks. Our solution based books give you the knowledge and power to customize the software and technologies you're using to get the job done. Packt books are more specific and less general than the IT books you have seen in the past. Our unique business model allows us to bring you more focused information, giving you more of what you need to know, and less of what you don't.

Packt is a modern, yet unique publishing company, which focuses on producing quality, cutting-edge books for communities of developers, administrators, and newbies alike. For more information, please visit our website: `www.packtpub.com`.

Writing for Packt

We welcome all inquiries from people who are interested in authoring. Book proposals should be sent to `author@packtpub.com`. If your book idea is still at an early stage and you would like to discuss it first before writing a formal book proposal, contact us; one of our commissioning editors will get in touch with you.

We're not just looking for published authors; if you have strong technical skills but no writing experience, our experienced editors can help you develop a writing career, or simply get some additional reward for your expertise.

[PACKT] PUBLISHING

Processing 2: Creative Programming Cookbook

ISBN: 978-1-84951-794-2 Paperback: 306 pages

Over 90 highly-effective recipes to unleash your creativity with interactive art, graphics, computer vision, 3D, and more

1. Explore the Processing language with a broad range of practical recipes for computational art and graphics
2. Wide coverage of topics including interactive art, computer vision, visualization, drawing in 3D, and much more with Processing
3. Create interactive art installations and learn to export your artwork for print, screen, Internet, and mobile devices

---

NumPy 1.5 Beginner's Guide

ISBN: 978-1-84951-530-6 Paperback: 234 pages

An action-packed guide for the easy-to-use, high performance, Python based free open source NumPy mathematical library using real-world examples

1. The first and only book that truly explores NumPy practically
2. Perform high performance calculations with clean and efficient NumPy code
3. Analyze large data sets with statistical functions
4. Execute complex linear algebra and mathematical computations

Please check **www.PacktPub.com** for information on our titles

[PACKT] PUBLISHING

R Graph Cookbook

ISBN: 978-1-84951-306-7 Paperback: 272 pages

Detailed hands-on recipes for creating the most useful types of graphs in R-starting from the simplest versions to more advanced applications

1. Learn to draw any type of graph or visual data representation in R
2. Filled with practical tips and techniques for creating any type of graph you need; not just theoretical explanations
3. All examples are accompanied with the corresponding graph images, so you know what the results look like
4. Each recipe is independent and contains the complete explanation and code to perform the task as efficiently as possible

---

Pentaho Data Integration 4 Cookbook

ISBN: 978-1-84951-524-5 Paperback: 352 pages

Over 70 recipes to solve ETL problems using Pentaho kettle

1. Manipulate your data by exploring, transforming, validating, integrating, and more
2. Work with all kinds of data sources such as databases, plain files, and XML structures among others
3. Use Kettle in integration with other components of the Pentaho Business Intelligence Suite

Please check **www.PacktPub.com** for information on our titles

10107545R00042

Made in the USA
San Bernardino, CA
09 April 2014